Stunning

and Other Plays

Stunning

and Other Plays

David Adjmi

THEATRE COMMUNICATIONS GROUP   NEW YORK   2011

Stunning and Other Plays is published by Theatre Communications Group, Inc.,
520 Eighth Avenue, 24th Floor, New York, NY 10018-4156

The publication of *Stunning and Other Plays* through TCG's Book Program
is made possible in part by the New York State Council on the Arts with the
support of Governor Andrew Cuomo and the New York State Legislature.

TCG books are exclusively distributed to the book trade by Consortium Book
Sales and Distribution.

CIP data information is on file at the Library of Congress, Washington, DC.

Book design, composition and cover design by Lisa Govan

First Edition, October 2011

Contents

Stunning

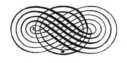

Special Thanks

(In no order) Rebecca Taichman, Lisa Portes, Morgan Jenness, Mark Subias, Adam Greenfield, Polly Carl, Stephen Willems, New York Theatre Workshop, Paige Evans, André Bishop, Emily Shooltz, Dartmouth College, Danny Mastrogiorgio, Quincy Tyler Bernstine, Laura Heisler, Charlayne Woodard, Cristin Milioti, Michael Goodfriend, Gabrielle Fernandez-Coffey, Abby Wood, Clint Brandhagen, Lecy Goranson, Jeanine Serralles, Steve Rattazzi, Sas Goldberg, Nilaja Sun, April Yvette Thompson, Howard Shalwitz, Elissa Goetschius, Miriam Weisfeld, Woolly Mammoth Theatre Company, Kathy Sova, Paul Rusconi, Heidi Schreck, Kip Fagan, Jim McCarthy, Gloria Peterson, Anne Kauffman, Tory Stewart, Kath Tolan, Philip Himberg and all my friends at Sundance, Olivier Sultan, Corinne Hayoun. And to all the actors who participated in countless readings, workshops, etc., of this play who weren't mentioned here. Thank you.

Production History

Stunning was developed by New York Theatre Workshop (James C. Nicola, Artistic Director; William Russo, Managing Director) and Manhattan Theatre Club (Lynne Meadow, Artistic Director; Barry Grove, Executive Producer). The world premiere was produced in Washington, DC, by Woolly Mammoth Theatre Company (Howard Shalwitz, Artistic Director; Jeffrey Herrmann, Managing Director) on March 10, 2008. It was directed by Anne Kauffman; set design was by Daniel Conway, costume design was by Helen Q. Huang, lighting design was by Colin K. Bills, sound design was by Ryan Rumery; the dramaturg was Miriam Weisfeld, the dialect coach was Sasha Olinick and the production stage manager was Rebecca Berlin. The cast included:

LILY	Laura Heisler
BLANCHE	Quincy Tyler Bernstine
IKE	Michael Gabriel Goodfriend
SHELLY	Gabriela Fernandez-Coffey
JOJO	Clinton Brandhagen
CLAUDINE	Abby Wood

Stunning was produced at Lincoln Center Theater (LCT3; André Bishop, Artistic Director; Bernard Gersten, Executive Director; Paige Evans, Director of LCT3) in June 2009. It was directed by Anne Kauffman; set design was by David Korins, costume design was by Miranda Hoffman, lighting design was by Japhy Weideman, sound design was by Rob Kaplowitz; the stage manager was Megan Schwarz. The cast included:

LILY	Cristin Milioti
BLANCHE	Charlayne Woodard
IKE	Danny Mastrogiorgio
SHELLY	Jeanine Serralles
JOJO	Steven Rattazzi
CLAUDINE	Sas Goldberg

Characters

LILY SCHWECKY: Cute, slight, naifish, something of an oddball. The "baby"—she's sixteen going on about eleven; she's a bit regressed. Her mind works quickly but her thoughts are incredibly scattered. A follower, but it's more out of a need for connectedness than an innate passivity.

BLANCHE NESBITT: Lily's new housekeeper. African American; an extremely intelligent, voluble and terribly sensitive autodidact. Damaged, but maintains a great sense of irony and dry humor. She adapts to survive—she's performative, and the performance wears her down eventually. An outsider. Forties.

IKE SCHWECKY: Lily's new husband. Controlling, brute, bumptious, but there's something fragile in him, broken—he's more transparent than he thinks. Mid-forties.

SHELLY: Lily's big sister. A leader; she's got a stentorian quality, but naturalizes this by cultivating "girly" preoccupations. The laziness of her r's and a's feels calculated and somehow hostile. Early twenties.

JOJO: Shelly's uxorious husband. Basically a good guy but limited; rather put upon, has trouble sticking to his guns. Thirties/early forties.

CLAUDINE: A bit hysterical; unselfconscious—even brutish—in her bids for approval. She has a desperate conformity. Nineteen.

Setting

The play takes place largely within the confines of the Midwood section of Brooklyn—a very affluent, largely Jewish area; one that exerts a centripetal force on the people who live there. Despite the proximity to Manhattan, there's a provincialism to it, an insularity, but also an extremely tight-knit sense of community.

Time

Early 2000s.

Set

I know three things about the set for this play: (1) Continuing the homage to Douglas Sirk and Tennessee Williams (and Plato too, from *The Republic*), mirrors are very important to this world. It would not be out of keeping with the tenor of the play (and the themes of illusion, imitation, deception, whatever) to *selectively* stage whole scenes, parts of scenes, sections of the stage using full-length mirrors (think *Las Meninas* or even *The Lady from Shanghai*), keeping in mind, obviously, that this can't be used egregiously. (2) The world of the play is bleached-out, whitewashed—there's no color in it save for various shades of white and transparent surfaces, glass, mirrors, etc. (3) The set should have some kind of motility: it isn't stable; it wants to move, it wants to transform, whether with panels, walls, rollers, I'm not sure, but perspectives can shift.

Costumes

Monochromes. Of course Lily, Ike and JoJo (and eventually Blanche) are garbed in "JoJo Jeans" for much of the play—but there's not much color. Blanche's clothes should be, conversely, boldly colorful, but—like Rothko's canvasses—get darker or more charged as the play progresses.

Note on Style

The play shifts styles. While it is concerned with psychological reality, it only *intermittently* correlates with the detail or psychological consistency usually associated with Realism. There are deliberate *and drastic* alternations in tone, style, etc., that happen scene by scene, within scenes and *between beats* with *no* transition. It is therefore *critical* for actors to follow the rhythms of the play, as it is scored; the psychological truth can be extracted from this.

It is crucial that the shifts and transitions in the piece, no matter how abrupt, are rooted in an emotional reality.

Note on Text

A double slash (//) indicates either an overlap or a jump—i.e., no break between the end of one character's speech and the beginning of the following speech (thanks Caryl Churchill).

Speech in parentheses indicates either a sidetracked thought—or footnote—within a conversation, or a shift in emphasis with *no* transition.

A [STOP] is a *(Pause)* followed by either a marked shift in tone or tempo (like a cinematic jump-cut or a quantum leap) or *no* change in tempo whatsoever—somewhat like putting a movie on *(Pause)* and then pressing play. These moments in the play are less psychological than energetic. They have a kind of focused yet unpredictable stillness, something akin to martial arts, where there is preparedness in the silence. Where a lunge or a swift kick can be delivered from seemingly out of nowhere: quickly, invisibly. Where the energy can shift dramatically in a nanosecond.

Glossary of Syrian-American Terms

ABOOSE: "Oh how sweet and adorable."

CA-AN ("ca" as in "cat" and "an" as in "ann"): Spoken when challenging the veracity of something. Has a vaguely sarcastic connotation, as in, "Yeah, right!" Sometimes serves as phatic punctuation.

DIBEH: Slang for idiot (female); dib (male).

ERT: An exclamation of disgust or revulsion.

GAZZCASE ("a," as in "lair"): Playful term for someone who is mentally disorganized, a kind of screwball.

GAZZY: Silly and fun.

GIMMETHEBOSSES: "Give me a kiss."

HEEE: Not a word but a sharp intake of breath indicating shock, concern, surprise or worry.

IBE (with a hard "i," silent "e"): Comment on "shameful" or inappropriate behavior.

OBDEH ("ob" as in "obverse"): Person of African descent (female); obid (male).

OOLIE: An exclamation of shock, worry, horror, discovery—and spoken with correlative intonations (reverential worry: "*ooooollllliiieeeee*," "OO!LIE!," "*OOLIE!*" etc.).

SHOOF, SHOOFIE: A command—"Look!" As in, "Shoof haddie!" ("Look at her!")

SKETCHING: Slang for kidding or joking.

The history of the world is not the theater
of happiness.
Periods of happiness are blank pages in it.

—G. W. HEGEL, *PHILOSOPHY OF HISTORY*

Act One

The Ambassadors

1.

Claudine's house.
A card game.
Three girls sitting at a card table: Shelly, Lily, Claudine.
They all have nearly identical feathered hair modeled after the '70s "Farrah" look from Charlie's Angels. *They all have bangles—meretriciously* loud *bangles—on their wrists; this is an index of wealth.*
They all have variations of the same boots, clothes—one gets the sense that no one does anything in this world without the tacit agreement of the others.
Lily is painfully, comically sunburnt and peeling for most of this act.
The play opens with a virtuosic shuffling of the cards.
Rapid fire:

SHELLY: Stick to the rules //
LILY: Where's // Tuni?

SHELLY: Jacks or better nothing wild everybody // in?

LILY: We have to wait for Tuni but-h.

CLAUDINE: Tuni's not coming she's getting a divorce:

SHELLY: She's //

CLAUDINE: Ye you didn't // hear she's

SHELLY: Whaddayou*sketching*? //

CLAUDINE: separating from (no-I'm-not-sketching) she's sep-
arated // from

LILY: Oolie! //

SHELLY: She just got married!

LILY: She had a baby //

CLAUDINE: YE and the baby I think it has like a Down's
syndrome?

SHELLY: HEEE //

CLAUDINE: (Aduknow) //

LILY: And she //

CLAUDINE: (or like) //

SHELLY: I //

CLAUDINE: *and they hid it* //

SHELLY *(To Lily)*: (Stop-playing-with-your-hands) //

CLAUDINE: and Tuni had to take it in to see a *specialist* //

LILY: Wheh?

CLAUDINE: in the *ity-cay* This *y-gay* //

SHELLY: (You're-making-me-nervous-stop-it) //

CLAUDINE: (I think it was Mount Sinai) //

SHELLY *(Fixes earring)*: (I-had-my-transplant-theh) //

CLAUDINE: And like the husband // like

(Shelly pulls a packet of juicy fruit, puts down the cards.)

LILY: Did she have a // girl?

CLAUDINE: he like //

LILY *(Imagining a cute baby)*: Aboose.

SHELLY *(To Claudine)*: (You want?)

CLAUDINE: And then I (no-it's-not-sugahless) and I think he
was rejecting the kid // or

(Lily accepts a stick of gum, chews.)

SHELLY: I thought //

CLAUDINE: or no, YEAH // and he

LILY: Heeee //

CLAUDINE: goes "I don't want *you*? and I don't want this *kid*? and // gimme a divorce"

LILY: With the *Down's* syndrome // *kid*?!

SHELLY: Dib Who's the husband.

CLAUDINE: Morris Betesh //

SHELLY: Piece a shit.

CLAUDINE: No-Ye-He-is-a-piece-//-a-shit

LILY: Who's he related to?

CLAUDINE: Schweckies of Avenue P.

SHELLY: That's not a good // family

CLAUDINE *(Munching violently on a carrot stick)*: *Piece a shit* //

LILY: Do they own Duane Reade? //

SHELLY: THAT'S YA SECOND COUSIN DUANE READE //

CLAUDINE *(Vicious)*: *They have a bad* // *reputation*

LILY: What do they own //

CLAUDINE *(Finger wagging tone)*: Bad family //

SHELLY: And I go to her I go //

CLAUDINE *(Vicious)*: BAD //

SHELLY: I go don't marry this jerk //

CLAUDINE: Me too!

SHELLY: (And-remembah?!-and-I-go) //

CLAUDINE: Me-*too*-everyone-her-mother-*Debby* //

SHELLY: and now she's // screwed

CLAUDINE: And-I-//-go:

SHELLY: fogettaboutit //

CLAUDINE *(Shaking her hand as if it's burned)*: Yeah-*oh-figget*-//-*it*

SHELLY *(Miminking her hand shaking)*: *Ooooolie figetiiiiiiit* //

CLAUDINE: (She // screwed herself)

SHELLY: She's // finished

CLAUDINE: She committed // suicide

LILY: (Oolie!) //
CLAUDINE: RUINED!!

[STOP]

(Crunching a carrot stick) I like the dip What's in this //
LILY: Chives
CLAUDINE *(Bright)*: Heeee: I *like* chives. //
LILY: Should we // play?
CLAUDINE *(Quick)*: (Did you see Debbie's haih? She cut // it)
SHELLY: I like your bangles //
LILY *(Exhibiting her wrist)*: Sheri-got-me-for-my-showah
CLAUDINE *(Muffled resentment)*: Your wrist looks thin.
LILY: I gained weight-h //
SHELLY: Ca-an she's a *stick*!
CLAUDINE *(A little too loud)*: You're BLACK!
SHELLY: She's a Obdeh. //
LILY: From the panama jack.
CLAUDINE: *Obdeh*
SHELLY: She always // gets black
CLAUDINE *(Singsong)*: HOW WAS ARUBA-AAAAA?
LILY: Stunning.
SHELLY *(Singsong)*: Ye-eee-eeeee?
CLAUDINE: Dibeh-you-nevah-said-nothing-You-got-back-when:
LILY: Yestiday //
CLAUDINE: (Ack-blay) //
SHELLY: You flew delta? //
LILY: United.
SHELLY: WITH THE TERRORISTS—ah?!
CLAUDINE: LEAVE HAH.
SHELLY: Whatditellyou:
LILY: Ikey bought the // tickets, I
CLAUDINE: You look STUNNING.
SHELLY *(Chews gum efficiently)*: (Mommy wants you // to cawl hah)
CLAUDINE: You look UNNING-STAY.

SHELLY: cawl hah // cell
LILY *(Juts out her arm)*: *I'm peeling: shoof*
CLAUDINE: Was the sand pink. //
LILY *(Peels an enormous swatch of skin)*: SHOOFIE.
CLAUDINE: HEEEE. Put // cream!
SHELLY *(Mean)*: Dibeh ya hafta put cream!
LILY: I put-h!!
CLAUDINE: Is the house finished Wheh's Ikey?
LILY: We just moved in //
CLAUDINE: Did you go jetskiing? //
LILY: The water was choppy //
CLAUDINE: But-it's-fun-right-isn't-it-I-TOLD-YOU-right //
LILY: I //
CLAUDINE: Isn't it I know.

[STOP]

SHELLY: You're *egnant-pray?*
LILY *(Wide-eyed)*: Aduknow.
SHELLY: Ca-an.
LILY: He wants to start // soon.
CLAUDINE: Is the house finished //
SHELLY: Excited?
LILY: Ye.
CLAUDINE: I want kids.
SHELLY: You'll have-h!
CLAUDINE: I'm sick of living with my mothah.
SHELLY: I told you I would set you up
CLAUDINE: with *Stevie* //
LILY *(Revulsion)*: Ert //
CLAUDINE: THIS IS HOW HE DANCES //
SHELLY: He comes from a good // family.
CLAUDINE *(Practically hyperventilating)*: I'm nineteen-h! //
LILY *(Gingerly)*: Ya bracelet is shahp
CLAUDINE: (My-cousin-makes-bracelets-she-sells-them-at-flea-
    markets.)

SHELLY *(Blame)*: You don't go to parties //

CLAUDINE: YOU SOUND LIKE *MY MOTHAH.*

SHELLY: Do guys like whiney girls NO.

CLAUDINE *(Covers her face, emotionally exhausted)*: I'm old.

LILY: (I feel old.)

CLAUDINE: Bonnie has four kids //

SHELLY: (Three) //

CLAUDINE: And she's two years younger than me I'm gonna
     be twenny.

LILY: If I met someone you will.

CLAUDINE: But you're pretty.

LILY: You're stunning!

CLAUDINE: I'M FAT!

LILY: Look at my // calves

CLAUDINE *(Looking in a mirrored surface)*: No-I-have-//-
     crows-feet

SHELLY *(Reapplying lipstick)*: I like your // oots-bay

LILY: I'm // fat

CLAUDINE: (I got those at Loehmann's) //

LILY: I feel old.

CLAUDINE: SHUT UP YA FREAKIN TWELVE-ah.

LILY: I'm seventeen next week.

[STOP]

CLAUDINE: I feel more secure in myself; don't you think I'm
     more secure in myself than I was this time lastchyee //

LILY: I like your bracelet //

CLAUDINE: *(Errrrrt, I hate* this bracelet, it's dis*gu*sting.)

SHELLY: How's the house?

LILY: Big.

CLAUDINE: I heard it's stunning

(Beat.)

LILY: There's a ghost.

SHELLY: Whadayou *tawking* about?
LILY: Ikey said there was, and then I saw it the other night.

(Short pause.)

SHELLY: There's no ghost.

(Pause.)

LILY: I saw it. *(Beat; then to Shelly)* I miss Mommy and Daddy.
SHELLY: Don't be such a freakin baby.

(Beat.
Lily, somewhat abstracted, lifts her thumb to her mouth,
grazing the tip of her lip; Shelly sees this—pushes it back
down in her lap.)

(Regaining awareness) It's weird. Aduknow.

[STOP]

CLAUDINE: I saw Stevie on the holiday I saw Stevie I saw Ral-
phie // I saw
SHELLY: Are we gonna play or what.
CLAUDINE: Three card draw.
LILY: Deal //
SHELLY: (Five.)
CLAUDINE *(To Lily, regarding some pastry)*: Pass that—

(Loud music cuts her off.)

2.

Lily and Blanche.
An interview.
Lily and Ike's home in Midwood, Brooklyn.

The house is all white—perhaps several shades of white, but white. There is no color in this set.
The minimalism Lily espouses is that of the arid, philistine, nouveau riche—no art or anything—but terribly impressive in its own bombastic right.
A vase of dilapidated chrysanthemums in a vase on a mantel.
Lots of reflective surfaces.
A fishbowl with a lonely confused little goldfish swimming in circles—a single charged node of color in an otherwise color-less room.
Lily has a checklist in hand. Blanche stands out like a sore thumb.

LILY: What's your name?
BLANCHE: Blanche.
LILY *(Quizzical)*: Isn't that something you do to vegetables?
BLANCHE: I don't cook: //
LILY *(Mild suspicion)*: Do you do windows?
BLANCHE: (Yeah and I iron) //
LILY *(Vague panic)*: Tennis skirts?
BLANCHE *(Desperate retraction)*: *But I could learn to //* cook
LILY: (Because-they're-white-and-if-you-burn-them-I'll-freak.)
BLANCHE: I won't.

(Beat.)

LILY: Are you detail-oriented?
BLANCHE: Uh-huh.
LILY: Like "orientated towards the details"?
BLANCHE *(Nonplussed)*: (Isn't that what that // means?)
LILY: I play tennis Wednesdays and Fridays //
BLANCHE *(Chummy)*: Oh I used to play *squash* //
LILY *(Unbroken sentence)*: It's good for this *(Points to arm)* feel this *(Gestures)* it's a great spoht tennis.
BLANCHE *(Feeling and talking at the same time)*: But that was a long time ago.
LILY *(Points to hip)*: It's good for this.

BLANCHE: (Supple) //

LILY: But my backhand is suffering //

BLANCHE: *Pity* //

LILY: And you have to use bleach! I'm very meticulous about everything and I have ways I like things done; I like things a certain way, I'm meticulous. *(Aimlessly sprinkles fish food)* "Hiiiiiiiieeee" *(To Blanche; still sprinkling)* that's Kitty // it gets fed once

BLANCHE *(Looks for a cat)*: Where?

LILY: in the morning—"hiiiiii" (But-don't-overfeed-it-cuz-you'll-kill-it.)

BLANCHE: The *fish*?

LILY: Kitty—I know it's funny right? It's *gazzy*—it's from Anne *Frank*? That's her diary, did you ever read that book?

BLANCHE *(The whole thing is too much for her)*: Uh.

LILY: She kept a *diary*?

[STOP]

(She forgets what she was saying. She jingles her bangles. Beat.)

So-whatevah. *(Resuming her checklist)* Do you know // how to

BLANCHE: Forgive me but I thought I had this job already.

(Beat.)

LILY: What-h.

BLANCHE: This feels like an interview.

(Beat.)

LILY *(Indignant)*: Well I thought you would be Porto-*Rican*!

(She pulls her gum out and makes shapes with it.)

BLANCHE: Why'd you think that.

LILY *(Darts a look)*: *Because we wanted a Porto-RICAN-h.*

(She pops the gum back in her mouth.)

BLANCHE: I'm confused.

LILY: I don't think this is gonna work out, lemme call you a car service.

(She goes to the phone, dials.)

BLANCHE: But I have all my luggage with me.

LILY: Wheh do you live.

BLANCHE *(Panicked)*: *Don't do that.*

LILY: I have a carry thing *(Into phone)* Always Available? I need a cahr.

BLANCHE: Please don't call me a cab // I don't

LILY: Do you want to take the train?

BLANCHE *(We can see the despair)*: I'd . . . prefer. I. I don't have anywhere to *go.*

LILY: I'm more comfortable around Porto-Ricans. *(Into phone)* Hello?

BLANCHE: LISTEN: I don't have anywhere to *go* and I'm *ti*red, can't you just try me // out

LILY *(Into phone)*: 929 Ocean Parkway, it's between—

(Blanche grabs the phone, hangs it up.)

BLANCHE *(Verging on tears)*: I DON'T HAVE ANYWHERE TO *GO!*

[STOP]

LILY: Ya giving me a headeeche.

(Beat.)

BLANCHE *(Manages a smile)*: Sorry.

(Beat.)

LILY: Ya meeking me very nervous-h.
BLANCHE: I'm—sorry. I'm . . .

> *(Blanche straightens up a few things to palliate—she as-sumes the comportment of some housekeeper Lily may have seen on television; she plasters on a smile. Lily, vaguely soothed, produces a nail file.)*

LILY *(Files her nails; bright)*: It's just I had Porto-Ricans my whole life, as maids? My mother had a Porto-Rican maid? and then when I was a little girl I had a maid called Anna Maria. She took care of me; I loved hah: she taught me *Spanish*? she took me to the *park*, and pushed me on the swing—*ella me decia: "Lily tú eres un angel, y tu pelo es de ceda // te quiero como mi hija"*
BLANCHE: *¡¡Yo-tambien-te-puedo-mecer-en-el-columpio-vamos-al-parque-AHORA-MISMO!!*

(Beat.)

LILY *(Shocked, ecstatic, drops nail file)*: *¡¡¡¡¿¿TU HABLAS ESPAÑOL!!!!??*
BLANCHE: (I studied languages.)
LILY: *Do you want a piece a gum? //*
BLANCHE: *Gracias!*

(They chew gum and look at each other.)

LILY: I've been chewing this same gum for three days.
BLANCHE: That's a lot of gum.
LILY *(Quick)*: It is? No it's not because it's just one piece: I been *chewin* it fa three days. *Heeeee*: I *love* gum, you know what I like, charms blow pops: OH MY GAWD. I used to

get in so much *trouble?* in my *math* class? Oh my od-gay the *rabbi?* HEEEEEEE: because you're not allowed to chew gum? and he caught me? and I was gonna swallow it and I didn't? and he stuck it in my HAIH!!! *Ha ha ha ha ha.* Oh my goawd he was SO. SICK.

BLANCHE: Did //

LILY: Rabbi-Lerner-he's-SICK-oh-my-god-I-LOVE-him.

BLANCHE: You're in school?

LILY: Me no I quit //

BLANCHE: You // did?

LILY: Lastchyee, because I got married. I wanted to stay but my mother told me quit. Anyway I had a lot of planning with the wedding and everything.

BLANCHE *(Pretending it's all normal)*: How long have you been married?

LILY: I had a long engagement.

BLANCHE: How long?

LILY: Three years.

BLANCHE: Wow

LILY: I was twelve!

(Beat.)

BLANCHE: When you—got *engaged?*

LILY *(Filing nails)*: Ye.

BLANCHE *(Incredulous)*: You're *fifteen?*

LILY: Seventeen Well I'm gonna be My birthday's next week.

BLANCHE: But you said three years.

LILY: (I mis-did the math) We're goinna Tavern on the *Green!*

BLANCHE: That's quite a young age to be married.

LILY: What? Yeah. No. But I'm mature. *(Contemplative)* I matured very fast starting when I was ten? I'm more matured since then, I was ten then I was a kid, I'm more matured now.

BLANCHE: Is that some kind of religious custom? To get married so young?

LILY: We're Jewish.

BLANCHE: You don't look Jewish.

LILY: How do I look?

BLANCHE: Middle Eastern.

(Beat.)

LILY *(Perplexed and annoyed)*: Middle *Eastin*!!??

BLANCHE: You have Middle Eastern features. You know Dark Features?

LILY *(Squinting in disbelief)*: I'm *tan*. I went to *Aruba*? //

BLANCHE: Not your complexion, your *features*.

LILY: I look *white*.

BLANCHE: Not to me.

LILY *(Indignant)*: What do you mean not to you, *look at me* //

BLANCHE: I'm lookin.

(A brief staring contest.)

LILY *(Sheepish)*: Well my family *they* are . . . I think from . . . the Middle East.

(Beat.)

BLANCHE: Where? //

LILY: Aduknow *the Middle East somewheh!*

BLANCHE: You don't know where?

(Beat.)

LILY: I think Syria.

BLANCHE: I didn't know there were Syrian // Jews.

LILY: But we're all *white*.

BLANCHE: Well technically you *aren't* white if // you

LILY: I tan easy? I have melanin in my skin?

(Beat. Then playing along:)

BLANCHE: *That's a nice tan.*

LILY: I'm peeling! *(She gleefully peels a huge rectangle of skin off her arm)*

BLANCHE *(Horrified)*: You should use lotion for that!

LILY: *I use!* //

BLANCHE: Black people use cocoa butter, that's why we don't get any wrinkles //

LILY: (I'm getting // wrinkles)

BLANCHE: You know that expression "black don't crack"?

LILY: No.

BLANCHE: That's where that's from.

LILY: You don't have any wrinkles.

BLANCHE: I know and I'm forty-three.

LILY *(Grabbing onto the sofa)*: HEEEE: THAT'S FREAKIN OLD.

BLANCHE *(Disconcerted)*: It's not *that* old.

LILY: (But-you-don't-look-it.)

BLANCHE *(Pridefully)*: "Black don't crack."

LILY: Cocoa butter.

BLANCHE: And you're *not* getting // *wrinkles*

LILY: And your skin loses collagen That's what happens when you get old.

BLANCHE: Not you, you got great skin.

LILY: Your skin loses elastin, that's what happens, it's called elastin. *(She goes up to the mirror and examines her "wrinkles" while speaking)* So when people come to my house I want things to appear a certain way, like I want everything to be spotless—you see how everything is white that's how I want things to be Stunning stunning *white* //

BLANCHE: Does this mean I have // the job?

LILY: And we have a bucket of paint in every room So if things start to get dirty like if there's spots? like on the walls? or if you have nothing to do and there's down time you *repaint* OK?

BLANCHE *(Sigh of relief)*: *Thank you.*

LILY: Can I call you Anna Maria?

BLANCHE: Why? //

LILY: I just like that name //

BLANCHE: I was hoping you'd call me Ms. Nesbitt //

LILY: *Who's that?* //

BLANCHE: Me.

(*Beat.*)

LILY: I-kinda-hoped-I-could-call-you-Anna-Maria (is-that-*okaaaay*-I-feel-//-*baaaad*)

BLANCHE: I // kinda

LILY (*Regressing*): Anna-Maria-you're-so-nice-Anna-MARIA.

(*She hugs Blanche. She claps a tiny clap.*)

BLANCHE: Where's my room?

LILY (*Cheerful*): It's in the basement!

BLANCHE: And it's safe?

LILY (*Wide-eyed cheer*): We took the asbestos out of the *ceiling*!

BLANCHE: Oh good (?)

LILY: There's an alarm //

BLANCHE: OK.

LILY: (Could you not track // dirt?)

BLANCHE: (I'll take these // off)

LILY (*Single breath*): When you're finished unpacking you can dustbust The kitchen's just around theh? you turn right and it's right there OK? I'm gonna get a facial here's my cell if you need it Oh wait I don't have a pen.

BLANCHE (*Fear*): And I have the job right?

LILY (*Scrunches her face in the mirror*): (I'm losing elastin.)

BLANCHE: (You look // fine)

LILY: OOLIE! I'm going to be late for my manicuah //

BLANCHE: *OK.*

LILY (*Frantically grabbing her things*): Down the stairs and the first door on your left That's your room.

BLANCHE: Down // the—
LILY: No second //
BLANCHE: What //
LILY: Door //
BLANCHE: On my left? //
LILY: *No right.*

(*Blanche descends the stairs, hauling her heavy luggage with her.*)

(*Chatters away in Spanglish after her*) Oh and be careful, the steps Let me show you It's very steep. (*Spanish, speaks quickly*) *Todavía estamos trabajando Anna Maria la luz está a tu derecha.* (*Runs after her*) Switch the alarm off, *cuidado Anna Maria* careful don't fall . . . ANNA MARIA!!!!

(*She looks after Blanche descending the stairs, her eyes glowing preternaturally.*
Arabic music cuts in.)

3.

JoJo and Ike.
They're both in fishing gear.
Both wear JoJo Jeans.
Ike has a button that reads: "I like Ike."
Lily is carrying an enormous fish that's nearly twice her size and weight.
Blanche is in the periphery, repainting the walls with a roller, a paint trough nearby.

IKE: You put it right on the grill //
LILY: With the bones?

JOJO *(Points)*: Don't debone // it

LILY: Ert.

IKE: Grilled whole fish you never had that It's // unreal

LILY: (I nevah had // that)

JOJO: That's what gives it flava.

LILY: I never cooked fish.

JOJO: You put lemon You put salt You put garlic //

IKE: You put fresh oregano //

JOJO: Mint //

IKE: No // mint

JOJO: MY FATHER PUT // MINT

IKE: YOU DON'T PUT MINT!

*(They roughhouse for a few seconds.
It ends just as suddenly as it started.)*

LILY: I'm taking lessons, cooking lessons, at the École, we're still on vegetables //

IKE: Gimmethebosses //

LILY: There's six kinds a // dice

IKE *(Kissing her paternally)*: (Gimmethebosses // gimmethebosses)

LILY: No seven, brunoise, something a "m"? Lemme // get my

IKE: ALRIGHTAREADY

LILY: What?!

IKE: WE'RE // HUNGRY

LILY: ARAAAIGHT!

[STOP]

(Ooof.)

(Lily exits, galled, lugging the huge fish.)

[STOP]

(The energy in the room shifts completely, becomes hyper-macho.
Tableau.)

JOJO: She p.g.? //
IKE *(Makes a muscle)*: Workin on it //
JOJO: Honeymoon? //
IKE: Feel //
JOJO: You're working out?
IKE: I joined the gym, Gold's, I work out six days a week //
JOJO: I hired a trainer //
IKE: I run five miles a // day
JOJO: I run six //
IKE: I do crunches //
JOJO: I do squats //
IKE *(Pointing finger)*: *You stretch?*
JOJO: I do bowflex //
IKE: *You wanna hurt your back?! //*
JOJO *(Points)*: (Don't point).

[STOP]

(Ike jogs in place.)

IKE: I'm in training.
JOJO: You gotta stretch the muscles.
IKE: I'm in pretty good shape // guy, my
JOJO: (Bowflex.)
IKE: age, look at Abie,
JOJO: Abie *yeah* // but
IKE *(Stops jogging)*: Look at my stomach Jo, *flat //*

(He lifts his shirt. JoJo, in examining his stomach, punches it.)

DID I SAY PUNCH?

[STOP]

JOJO: (Good definition.)
IKE: Flat //
JOJO *(Belated double take)*: (Wait-Abie-who?)
IKE *(Strikes an Atlas pose)*: Feel: //
JOJO: Whaddayouon*steroids*?
IKE *(Atlas pose two)*: Creatine.
JOJO: That's bad fa ya kidneys You want *kidney stones?*
IKE: *I don't got kidney stones ya douchebag //*
JOJO: *DOUCHEBAG //*

(Smack. Headlock. They get in Blanche's way.)

IKE: Uncle.
JOJO: NO!
IKE: I'll break ya fuckin neck.
BLANCHE: (I'll move.)

(Headlock. Blanche rolls her eyes.)

JOJO: UNCLE.

(Ike lets him out of the headlock.)

IKE: Power.
JOJO: Now my neck hurts //
IKE: Name of the game *(To Kitty)* Hiiiiiiiiiieeeeeeeeeee Kiiitty!

[STOP]

(Energy in the room shifts again completely: an extempore business meeting.)

JOJO: I'm hungry //

IKE *(Shift)*: *Alright let's talk business:* //

JOJO: *Alright* (lemme get my // pad)

IKE: *Shoof:* outsourcing //

JOJO: Tawk.

IKE: We're at a time of expansion We need to leverage our capabilities Increase our profit margin //

JOJO: I // already

IKE: I know you don't wanna do // it but

JOJO: And then we gotta bring more *people* in, I don't // wanna

IKE: LISTEN TA MAY—We expand the market, PR, advertising //

JOJO: No—

IKE: (Plus with decreasing the labor // costs)

JOJO: (It's-not-actually-so-much-cheaper-I-saw-the-spreadsheet.)

IKE: LISTEN TA MAY!

JOJO: I don't want no sweatshops, I'm not into that, *(He flexes some muscle)* Ibe.

IKE: They're not sweatshops,

JOJO: (I'm starving // where's the fish?)

IKE: These people need work, they're dropping like *flies,* they're being barbecued *alive* they NEED WORK //

JOJO: I //

IKE: You wanna be a nike You wanna be a godiva chocolate?

JOJO *(Points)*: JoJo Jeans!

IKE: JoJo JEANS //

JOJO *(Moves to sofa)*: And they got *sweatshops.*

IKE: (Who?)

JOJO: Nike, godiva, child *labor* //

IKE: My *grammotha* worked in child labor she freakin *oved-it-lay* //

JOJO: *CA-AN* //

IKE: "*CA-AN*" in a candy factory They gave her free candy bars //

JOJO: We already have a sizable profit margin.

IKE: What about our *skill set?*

JOJO: I //

IKE: We can leverage our capabilities CA-AN, Take it to the next level, we can be like a diesel, a levi's, a lee jeans (where's Brooke // Shields)

JOJO: I //

IKE: (Marky Mark The girl with the reversible mole) *not* this second-tier nonsense—if that's what you want fine I want MOAH!

JOJO: I want more // too.

IKE *(Practically edging him off the sofa)*: No cause you're lazy // *move*

JOJO: I'm // not

IKE: Spoiled bastard if (MOVE) if // you

JOJO: I'M NOT SPOILED //

IKE: SHADDAP (if-your-father-didn't-have-money-you'd-be-scraping-the-gutters-with-the-back-of-your-throat) //

JOJO: *What* //

IKE: SHADDAP (you're-too-lazy-to-even-understand-the-shit-life-you'd-have-if-you-weren't-so-spoiled) *That's* corruption //

JOJO: *I'm* corrupt? //

IKE: That's *repreHENsible* //

JOJO: I'M //

IKE: (You're-sitting-on-your-blackberry) // REPREHEN-SIBLE do

JOJO: (Wheh) //

IKE: you realize how much you have to work with Your *skill* set? Where's your ambition, where's your fire?—I'm like Vesuvius I'm like Magic Johnson I shoot hoops I have winged feet //

JOJO: I work my ass off. I *started* this company it's MY company //

IKE: ARE. YOU. IN?

(Pause.)

JOJO: You treat me like shit.
I'm your partner.

(*Pause.*)

IKE: I love you like a brother; you know that.

(*Beat.*)

JOJO: Yeah yeah.

(*Pause.*)

IKE (*Puts his arm around him*): Remember we picked up non-Jewish girls together?
JOJO (*Fond reminiscence*): The chick with bad teeth?
IKE: (Deltoids, traps, rhomboids)
JOJO: Fucked up teeth is hot . . .
IKE: Now we're *arried-may* //
JOJO: (She p.g. yet?)
IKE: I *told* // you
JOJO: "Be fruitful and // multiply"
IKE: I want ten // kids
JOJO: KILL THE PALE-FREAKIN-STINIANS //
IKE: (oneafteranothah-boom-boom-//-boom.)
JOJO (*Quick*): I says ta-hah: "YOUR BRA DON'T EVEN FIT-H" //
IKE: Who //
JOJO (*Quick*): She goes "I can't afford no bra" I go "I'll slip you twenty bucks if you show me your ass."
IKE: HA HA //
JOJO: HA HAHAHAH.

[STOP]

(*Beat; concession*) Arite //

IKE: YES?

JOJO (*A little lost, abstracted*): I don't know what I'm doing.

IKE (*Preening happily*): Cuz I'm alpha, cuz what I say goes, buddy

JOJO (*Violent*): BULLSHIT!

IKE: Alpha and the beta, the beginning and the end.

JOJO: (Omega.)

IKE: Who's got the power.

JOJO (*Regretting everything*): (I'm starved.)

IKE (*Posing in the mirror*): My arms are like *pistons.*

4.

Shelly and Lily.
They wear fila luxe tracksuits. Headbands too. Makeup: perfect. Lily is stretching her calves. Blanche is dusting inconspicuously in the periphery.

SHELLY: I used to get v's but now I do moons //

LILY: I have a French manicuah //

SHELLY: You go to Linear Nails? //

LILY: No I used to go theh.

SHELLY: With who Olga?

LILY: I don't go there // anymore.

SHELLY: Was she fat?

LILY: I go to Ana Orsini.

SHELLY: I used to go there.

[STOP]

LILY: I have a French manicuah.

(Shows her.)

SHELLY: Heeeee: Stunning.

LILY: Let me see your v's.

SHELLY: Moons.

LILY: I love // it-h

BLANCHE: Where's the pledge?

LILY: What.

BLANCHE: I'm dusting.

SHELLY: You use pledge? It gives you waxy buildup.

[STOP]

LILY: I thought //

SHELLY *(Harsh blame)*: You use pledge??

LILY *(Meek)*: Ye.

SHELLY *(To Blanche)*: LISTEN TA MAY: you don't use that, you wanna ruin all the furnitcha it's brand-new furnitcha very expensivo *mucho dinero*, you wanna ruin this?

(Blanche shakes her head.)

You don't use that on the furniture. *(To Lily)* Did you tell her about the floors?

LILY: I //

SHELLY *(To Blanche; eyeing her suspiciously)*: You be careful with the floors araight?

BLANCHE *(Restraint but it's difficult)*: What would you have me use.

SHELLY: *I can't remembah* it's this stuff // *(Snap, snap)*

LILY: Anna // Maria

SHELLY: *What's the freakin name? (Disproportionately angry) I CAN'T REMEMBAH. (Snap, snap)* It's much bettah.

[STOP]

BLANCHE: Well //

SHELLY: I'll have you call my girl My girl is very good She'll give you the name.

LILY *(After an uncomfortable spell)*: Did you get the invitation //
    for
SHELLY: Oh and I'm pregnant-h.

(Beat.)

LILY: *You're—*
SHELLY: The-baby's-fine-no-disfigurement-I-got-the-ultrasound-
    Tuesday.
LILY: HEEEEEE: SHEL // CONGRATS
SHELLY: (I saw a little hand I saw little feet.)
LILY: When did // you
SHELLY: I'm done with the first trimester they tell you not to
    tell anyone before that, I can still do exercise, speedwalk-
    ing aerobics: *am I glowing?* //
LILY: Ye //
SHELLY: (Badminton.)

(Beat.)

It's nice being pregnant just to glow.
LILY *(Twirling her hair)*: Did you tell Jo?
SHELLY: Yeah I mean no, I'll tell him, ca-an. Let's speedwalk.

(Beat.)

LILY: Do I?
SHELLY: What.
LILY: Glow.

(Beat.)

SHELLY *(Rhetorical)*: Are *you* pregnant?

*(Shelly smiles a freakishly wide, teasing smile at Lily;
pokes at her stomach.*

Blanche looks disdainfully at Shelly. Shelly stares her down. Blanche goes back to dusting, feigning interest in her dumb job.)

LILY: Let's speedwalk I have my thing.

(Shelly makes to leave. Hawklike, she watches Blanche, her mouth curled into a snarl.)

SHELLY: Shoof haddie.

(Lily looks up at Shelly who is still fixed on Blanche.)

SHOOFIE.

*(Lily jolts, looks to Shelly and then Blanche.
Blanche freezes a moment, then slowly pivots to see if she's being watched.
Shelly casually fingers the furniture for dust.)*

(Looks out casually) Ooday ooyay ink-thay ee-shay eels-stay?

(Blanche stops for a moment; Lily doesn't get it on the first try.)

LILY: Uht-way?
SHELLY: Do you think she *eels-stay?*
LILY *(Slightly embarrassed)*: I don't ow-knay.
SHELLY: SHOOFIE. *(Pause)* My *last* aid-may ole-stay ings-thay.

(Lily looks at her.)

(Whispers loudly) And she wasn't an *igger-nay.*

(Blanche freezes.)

LILY *(Deeply uncomfortable)*: When are we going already?
SHELLY: *Iggers-nay eel-stay.*

5.

Ike and Lily.
The master bedroom, night.
Ike does pushups on the floor. Lily watches him, bored.

IKE: Eighteen Nineteen.
LILY: She needs it to be off the books she said.
IKE: Twenny (sit-on-me) twenny-one.

(She gets on his back while he does pushups.)

LILY: She doesn't want to pay taxes.
IKE: So.
LILY: So she doesn't want a check, anyways I need money.
IKE: Don't I give you money?
LILY: I had to pay the gardener.
IKE: Twenny-seven.
LILY: And Frieda's shower, I had to get her // a present
IKE: You don't have enough money?
LILY: I //
IKE: Look at this house, you don't like this house?
LILY: (No I like it.)
IKE: Those are dolomite floors.
LILY: Shelly has a credit card.
IKE: Use Shelly's I'll give you the money.

(Lily stands.)

LILY: Could I have my own bank account?
IKE: We have a bank account (thirty-six).
LILY: My name's not on it.

IKE: Why do you need your name on everything.

LILY: My mother says that she never heard of a husband //
who won't

IKE: Your mother should mind her own business.

LILY: DON'T TURN ME AGAINST MY FAMILY.

[STOP]

(More pushups. She brushes her hair and cries.)

IKE: What the hell is wrong with you.

LILY: Aduknow.

IKE: Why are you *crying*?

LILY: I cry better than I speak.

IKE: Who says?

LILY: YOU.

(Beat. He produces cash.)

IKE: You need more I'll give you more.

LILY: I always need moah.

IKE: You buy gadgets.

LILY *(Gravitas)*: I need gadgets.

IKE: No one // needs

LILY: You don't know what I need.

(Ike stands.)

IKE: I don't know what you need?

(He grabs her. They kiss. It's not that sexy.)

That's a good girl.

*(She looks up at him with her big, watery eyes. She chews
her gum. She brushes her hair.)*

LILY: I'm bohed.

IKE: Your hair smells nice.

LILY *(Cheered)*: There's no flakes *right-h?*

IKE: Who's my little girl:

LILY: Me.

IKE *(Stroking her cheek)*: We'll talk about getting you a credit card.

LILY *(She sits on his lap)*: Also I want to take acting lessons.

IKE: You're already taking // lessons

LILY: At the École but that's cooking.

(Pause.)

IKE: I thought you wanted a family.

LILY: I can have // both

IKE: Because I want to have a family I thought that was clear.

(Beat.)

LILY: Maybe we // could

IKE: And I want it now //

LILY: But //

IKE: NOW I WANT IT NOW!

(He kisses her violently, starts tearing off her clothes. Blanche enters with laundry.)

BLANCHE: (Ooh I'll come back.)

(Blanche exits. Lily pulls away. Long pause.)

LILY: I got fitted for a diaphragm.

(Pause.)

IKE: Where is it.

(Beat.)

LILY: In the draw.
IKE: Get it.
LILY: I just thought in // case
IKE: GET IT.

(Pause. She goes to the drawer.)

Flush it.
LILY: But I . . . I just got it.

(Beat. He stares her down. She exits and returns.)

IKE *(Sweet)*: I didn't hear a flush.
LILY: You wanna check?
IKE: Don't use that tone with me.

(Chews her gum. Pops.)

LILY: We nevah do anything.
IKE: We just got back from Aruba.
LILY: I don't like being alone.
IKE *(Gleeful)*: You're not alone—you got the ghost!
LILY: You shouldn't have told me about that.
IKE *(Teasing)*: Awwwwwwww you scared of the ghost?
LILY: It's not funny //
IKE: BOO //
LILY: AAAAAAH

(She screams, he laughs.)

[STOP]

IKE: Honey there's no such thing as ghosts; don't be a dumb-bell.

(He ruffles her hair.)

LILY: You told me the real-estate guy said it was haunted.
IKE: You gonna listen to some real-estate guy?
LILY: You said you believed it.
IKE *(Gently, playful)*: Calm *down.*
LILY: I *saw* it. I saw it the other day. *(Beat)* I saw a face.

(Ike looks at her, smiling curiously.)

IKE: You saw a *ghost?*

(Beat.)

LILY: In the living room—the other day.

(Beat.)

IKE: Honey, you're just seeing things.
LILY *(Increasingly upset, a child's nightmare)*: It was looking right at me.

(He looks at her—he's a bit spooked.)

IKE: You saw somm?
LILY: The real-estate guy *told* you—I'm not making // it up
IKE: OK OK Look at me:
LILY: *I saw a face.*
IKE: Honey *look* at me.

(Lily looks at him.)

You think a ghost is gonna mess witchu when you got me protecting you?
LILY *(Sad)*: When are you leaving?
IKE: China? I told you, Thursday.

43

LILY: Are you going to be gone for my birthday?
IKE: I leave right after.
LILY: How long will you be gone?
IKE: A few weeks.
LILY: Can I come?
IKE: Business.

(*Pause. She goes to mirror, brushes her hair.*)

LILY: I'm not a dumbbell.

(*Beat.*)

IKE: Who's my little girl?

(*No answer.*)

(*Seducing her*) Daddy just has to be gone a little while and then he'll be home to take care of his baby.

(*Pause.*)

LILY (*Vulnerable*): I. I get panic attacks.
IKE (*Making fun of her*): "I get panic attacks."

(*Beat.*)

LILY (*Shocked by his cruelty*): It's not funny.
IKE (*Thinks this is funny*): AlrightAlright.

(*Beat.*)

LILY: I want to go with you.
IKE: Who's my little gadget?
LILY (*Frightened*): Don't leave.
IKE: Gimmethebosses.

6.

Blanche and Ike.
The kitchen. Morning.
Blanche has just made a pot of coffee, she's playing waitress.
Ike is eating—or slurping giant mouthfuls of cereal, alternat-
ing with drinking his creatine shake.

BLANCHE: Refill? //

IKE: Just a few things, you come in, not a big deal I was thinking Sunday //

BLANCHE: That's my day off.

IKE: (Get me some milk.)

BLANCHE: Right // but

IKE: Yeah but I need you to do it Sunday see because I have
   stuff going on so it has to be Sunday It's no big thing.

BLANCHE: You want me to come into your office //

IKE: Cuz we're moving, Hong Kong, stuff What's this?

BLANCHE: What? Oh. Soy milk.

IKE: I want regular milk.

BLANCHE: But have you tried // soy?

IKE *(Slams down milk, it spills)*: GET RID OF IT.

[STOP]

BLANCHE: But it's // very

IKE *(Petulant, shouting)*: I WANT MILK REGULAH MILK.

[STOP]

   Here's a sponge //

BLANCHE: I'll // clean it

IKE: (Where's-the-splenda-we-got-splenda?) //

BLANCHE: I //

IKE *(Bright)*: So this Sunday aright.

BLANCHE: Where?

IKE: The warehouse? It's in Jersey, Hoboken, I'll give you car-
fare I'll give you twenny bucks Don' worry about nothin //
BLANCHE: This is making me uncomfortable //
IKE: (Where's-the-splenda?) //
BLANCHE: Because. I, uh. I really don't clean offices?
IKE: You //
BLANCHE: Or. Well that's not what I was *hired* to do.

(He gives her a dirty look. Downs some creatine.)

(Increasingly nervous) And. And I . . . The *boundaries?*
(Beat) Do you see what I mean?
IKE *(Strained cheer)*: An office is a house but with file cabinets.
BLANCHE: But. It isn't *really* a house.
IKE: Pretend it's a house.
BLANCHE: But //
IKE *(Bright)*: Just pretend.
BLANCHE: Maybe we could organize it for later in // the week
IKE *(Violent)*: I'M-ASKING-YOU-TO-DO-ONE-THING!

*(Blanche, frightened, reflexively tries to shield herself. Ike
looks at her, completely unaware of his effect on her. Beat.)*

Whatsamatta?
BLANCHE: I— //
IKE: BOO!
BLANCHE *(Terrified)*: AHHHHHH!
IKE *(Delighted)*: I scahe ya? AH HAHAH.

(Blanche makes a feeble attempt to laugh along with him.)

Just do this for me, you're doing this for me. (I'll give you
twenny bucks.) *What kinda music izzat?*
BLANCHE: Rachmaninoff.
IKE: It's giving me a headache BAH BAH BAH.

(Blanche shuts it off.)

BLANCHE *(A concession)*: I used to work in an office; I did
  bookkeeping.
IKE: Good girl //
BLANCHE: I did a lot of office // jobs
IKE: You're gonna clean this up I gotta go.

(He gathers his things.)

You could make a lot of money bookkeeping, why don't
  you do that?
BLANCHE: Capitalism, cubicles, it's not for me.
IKE: But if you got *skills* Your *skill*set?
BLANCHE: Offices make me claustrophobic.
IKE: *Awffices?*
BLANCHE: The whole system.
IKE: Whaddayou a *commie?*
BLANCHE: Commie? No, more, uh //
IKE *(Checks out her booty)*: Commie //
BLANCHE: democratic socialist? anyway I resist labels //
IKE: (What are those, levi's?) //
BLANCHE: But the System wants to crush you.
IKE: "System"?
BLANCHE: The political truncheon? //
IKE: You got a good vocabulary.
BLANCHE: I got a PhD.
IKE: College, ye, not for me.
BLANCHE: I speak four languages.

(Beat.)

IKE: But there's only one language spoken in this world.

(He looks right at her.)

BLANCHE: Which is:

(Beat.)

IKE: Gold and Silver baby: Money talks. *(Beat)* That's right.

[STOP]

BLANCHE: Are you still // hungry?
IKE: And I don't want you wearing no levi's, *listen ta may*: I'll give you a closetful of jeans—the best—JoJo Jeans, a *closetful*. HOT. The *best*, you *listenna-may*.
BLANCHE: I don't got a closet.
IKE: Wha?
BLANCHE: My room, I use a suitcase.
IKE *(Preening)*: I'll get you a closet.
BLANCHE *(Irony)*: (Oo-that'd-be-nice.)
IKE: You like ya room?
BLANCHE *(Tense smile)*: Well-I feel-like-the-*walls*-are-closing-in-on-me-but-*yeah*.
IKE: You could take somethin for that.
BLANCHE *(Finessing)*: I'm a little claustrophobic aha // ha
IKE *(A bit too loud)*: YOU LIKE HIP-HOP!?
BLANCHE *(Jumps)*: I *yeah* I I like Tupac.
IKE: *Who?*
BLANCHE: They shot him? //
IKE: To me it's // noise
BLANCHE: (And Jay-Z got gunned down in that // video?)
IKE: I like it but it's noise //
BLANCHE: Well.

[STOP]

IKE *(Swaggering)*: You're a hip-hopster.
BLANCHE: I like Sibelius best.

(She watches him swagger. She doesn't know what to do.)

IKE *("Rapping")*:
    the hip
    the hop
    the hip hip hippity hop
    AND YOU DON'T STOP.

[STOP]

BLANCHE: Uh.
IKE: I know about hip-hop cause of my business, which is fashion Denim You like denim?
BLANCHE: It's—versatile.
IKE: You dress nice.
BLANCHE: Thanks.

(Blanche cleans.)

IKE: No I'm serious yo.

(Blanche cleans. Ike struts over.)

    Is that a hip-hop shirt?
BLANCHE: I don't know.
IKE: "FUBU: for us by us."
BLANCHE: Mm.
IKE: Like that.
BLANCHE *(Visibly uncomfortable)*: Yeah.
IKE: Nice.

(Beat.)

BLANCHE: You like Sibelius?
IKE: You like me?

[STOP]

(Seductive) You like me?

(He grabs her around the waist from behind. She carefully disentangles herself.)

BLANCHE: I'll get the dustbuster.

(She exits.)

7.

Lily, wearing her party dress, holds a few helium balloons tied together. She stares in the mirror. Blanche is reading by lamplight in the living room. She looks up from her book and sees a forlorn Lily.

BLANCHE: How was the party?
LILY: I'm old.
BLANCHE: Nice balloons.

(Lily plops down next to her, sighs dolefully.)

LILY: What are you reading?
BLANCHE: You wouldn't like this.
LILY: Could you read to me?
BLANCHE: It's theory.
LILY: What kinda theory? *(Grabs the book)* I din know you
   liked to read.
BLANCHE: Cause I'm a maid?
LILY: Ye.
BLANCHE: "Ye"?
LILY: YE!?!? *(Flipping through the book)* What kinda book is this?
BLANCHE: Semiotics. (Can I have that back?)
LILY: What's *semiotics-h*?

BLANCHE: The science of sign systems.

LILY: Why are you *reading* it?

(Lily flips through it.)

(Deeply offended) This is *retarded.*

BLANCHE: Well I have my degree in it. So. And I might have a teaching gig, I'm waiting to hear.

(Lily just looks at her, waits for the punch line.)

LILY *(Squinting)*: What *degree?*

BLANCHE *(Getting excited)*: I did my undergraduate work at Chicago? I studied lit with (well-minored-in-philosophy) but with Saul Bellow?

LILY: Saul—

BLANCHE: He won the Nobel Prize?

LILY: *Heeeee!*

BLANCHE: And Paul de *Man* all these *guys.* They're mostly dead now, but nice dead white guys. And I did graduate work at Brown in semiotics or—well under the rubric of critical // theory

LILY: What's *Brown?*

BLANCHE: A college.

LILY: Is it a black school?

BLANCHE: It's integrated.

LILY: With what?

(Beat.)

BLANCHE *(Confounded)*: White people (?)

LILY *(Scrunching up her face; indignant)*: So why's it called *Brown?*

BLANCHE: I think we should avoid racial issues

LILY *(Winsome)*: (I always avoid them) *So you went to college? That's so shaahp!*

BLANCHE: And I even had a thing with Cornel West; well it // wasn't—

LILY: Who //

BLANCHE: He used to send me these letters? like loveletters and shit and he's all frontin he's all "your eyes your hips" // And he's

LILY: Your teacher?

BLANCHE: He's like "I want to collapse you into the fold": I was like "*un*fold me."

LILY *(?)*:

BLANCHE *(Quick)*: Actually it's kinda ironic cuz I studied representations of the African-American Domestic in Mass Media with him and here I am—but I luuuv irony.

LILY: What's irony?

BLANCHE: This:

(She circles a finger to Lily and back.)

LILY: (Wha?)

BLANCHE: (Never mind.)

LILY: But if you went to college you can get a job—

BLANCHE: Well I need. I—I have to pay—my *loans.*

LILY *(Clapping)*: And you're my *maid?*

BLANCHE: For the time being.

LILY *(Sad)*: *But I don't want you to go.*

BLANCHE: But I might have this teaching job //

LILY *(Earnest)*: But-you-clean-my-house-*stunning* //

BLANCHE *(Produces pack of gum)*: Gum? //

LILY: *(Hee I love // dentyne.)*

BLANCHE *(Quick)*: And if I get it I can pay back my loans and it might lead to a tenure position Which can lead to making speeches and my book'll come out and I could maybe be a pundit Write for *Harper's* Start a blog—

LILY: Why couldn't you just get a teaching job to start with //

BLANCHE *(Defensive)*: DO YOU KNOW HOW HARD IT IS TO GET A TEACHING JOB?! *(Compensatorily girl-*

ish; quick) A-ha-ha I mean—no-but-the-academy is so *cloistered* I've applied for—I mean I cannot tell you how many jobs I've applied for—

LILY: Really?

BLANCHE: Oh I used reams of paper *reams* forests, whole *arbors*; but it's very white and it's hard as a black woman a lesbian I mean I like white guys *fine* but it's kind of a closed system and everyone wants to teach //

LILY: Why //

BLANCHE: Because what else are you gonna do with your worthless semiotics degree.!?!? *Aha-ha just kidding.* No but they love the whole ivory tower thing *knowamsaaayin?* Because you're insulated from the real world: *That's* the academy. They won't look at *reality.* And of course it's all worthless I mean really does anyone give a SHIT about synecdoche or Kant's epistemological turn? *No!* // And the academy

LILY: You want taffy?

BLANCHE: wants you to believe that the life of the mind, critical thinking, that this is *worth* something but—SURPRISE—it's just more hucksterism, another trick (yeah-gimme-a-taffy) "Oh *take* out two hundred grand in loans" (but it's all part of the capitalist // machinery)

LILY *(Proffering taffy)*: What's synecdoche? //

BLANCHE *(Chews taffy, blithe)*: But on the other hand people have *agency* //

LILY: (I like // taffy)

BLANCHE: It's like Helen Keller said "I am only one person but I'm still a person." //

LILY: (I thought she was mute) //

BLANCHE: (I'm paraphrasin) //

LILY: (Oh) //

BLANCHE: But it's the same shit over and over: Absolute power corrupts absolutely History repeats like a bad case a reflux: "History is a document of *barbarism*" //

LILY: Who said that? //

BLANCHE: (This-guy-who-wrote-his-major-works-on-toilet-paper-
because-he-was-a-political-//-prisoner)

LILY: (We're almost out of toilet // paper)

BLANCHE: (It's on my // list)

LILY: (Double ply) //

BLANCHE: *Yo me preocupo de esto //* cálmate

LILY: Wait: you're-a-*lesbian?*

BLANCHE: What.

(Beat.)

LILY *(A frisson):* I feel like I heard you say you're a . . . "es-
bian-lay."

BLANCHE *(Eating a taffy):* Yeah.

LILY: Yeah you *are* or yeah you *said* it?

BLANCHE: *Yeah* I said it cuz *yeah* I *am* it.

LILY: You're an actual "lesbian"?

BLANCHE *(Indignant):* No: I'm an optical illusion //

LILY: But like: don't you think that like the *girl?* is supposed
to go with the *guy?*

BLANCHE *(Playing dumb):* Why's that.

(Beat.)

LILY *(As if Blanche is mentally handicapped):* Because the
man? is *orientated* towards the *woman?*

BLANCHE: *Why?*

(Beat.)

LILY *(Unbridled frustration):* BECAUSE THE *GIRL?* IS
ORIENTATED? TOWARDS THE *GUY.*

BLANCHE: (Not this girl) //

LILY: (Adunundahstan) //

BLANCHE *(Only barely hiding her condescension):* Adrienne
Rich wrote an essay: that said that *all* women are lesbi-

ans. And there's a thing called: "compulsory heterosexuality"; and that first we're *all* dykes but it's the *system* that makes us straight.

LILY: What *system?*

BLANCHE: Forces of History Culture The usual vectors.

LILY: (Sounds like a dibeh) //

BLANCHE: (Well she aint.)

(Beat.)

LILY: Girls are supposed to have kids and get *married.* That's life.

BLANCHE: *No.* That's *your* life.

LILY: Uhhhhh: Ya not very *bright-h* if you can't see what I'm saying?

BLANCHE: Uhhhhh: Actually I graduated Phi Beta Kappa with a 3.94 GPA. Don't tell me I'm not *bright.*

(Pause.)

LILY: I just don't agree with your lifestyle.

BLANCHE: Well it's not up for *consensus.*

(Pause. Lily takes another tack.)

LILY: In the *Bible?*

BLANCHE *(Dismissive):* Yeah what do you know about the Bible?

LILY: Uhh: I read it like a *hundred* times!?

BLANCHE: Where?

LILY *(Vindication):* THE YESHIVAH!?!?

BLANCHE: (Yeah so you know the Bible What do you know) //

LILY *(Blunt textbook sanctimony):* LESBIANS IS WRONG //

BLANCHE: (And they taught you grammar // too Nice)

LILY: And I know about Sodom and Gomorrah!

BLANCHE: What do you know?

LILY: They were *Sodomites!*

BLANCHE: And:

LILY: And they had *sodomy ca-an?* And God said to Lot's wife not to look back and she looked back.

(Beat.)

BLANCHE: Would you look back?

LILY: God said no.

(Pause.)

BLANCHE *(Internal; faraway)*: I would.

(Lily looks at her.)

LILY: Fine but then you turn to a pillar of salt.

(Blanche turns to Lily.)

BLANCHE: You ever hear of a lose-lose proposition?

(Beat.)

(Somewhat portentous) No. Not yet. But you will.

(Silence.)

Well I have some reading to do so . . .

(Blanche goes back to her reading. Lily stares at her, glum.)

LILY: Should I go to college?

(Blanche turns a page, ignoring her. Lily continues to stare mercilessly. Blanche blocks out Lily's face with her hand.)

Maybe I shouldda finished high school. I wanted to stay but my mothah told me quit.

(Blanche forces a bright smile, clamps down on all her nervous energy; she makes a flash card.)

Do you think that's bad?

BLANCHE *(Dryest sarcasm)*: No, I think it's a stroke of genius.

LILY: So you think I // should

(Blanche whips around, looks right in her face.)

BLANCHE *(Terse)*: Honey, I can't fix you, I can't work out your problems for you!

LILY: I don't need you to // *fix* me.

BLANCHE: I can't control what you do!

LILY: But I wanna know what you *think* //

BLANCHE: I think we need a boundary, that's what I think.

(Blanche takes a breath, goes back to her book. Lily stares at her, chastened and a little offended. Lily tries to peek around the book, not getting the hint.)

LILY: I wanna go to college //

BLANCHE: Go //

LILY: I can't, Ikey wants to have kids, he said I have to start now. *(Genuinely sad)* And I'm really mad cause my diaphragm fit me good, and then he made me flush it down the toilet.

(Blanche looks up from her book, sees Lily upset. She shuts the book, agitated, gets her things together.)

BLANCHE: I'm going to bed.

LILY: What's a matter?

BLANCHE: What's a matter, you're making some really bad choices and now I gotta sit here and watch you ruin your life and I don't wanna be involved, OK? *I told you that!*

(Lily looks at her, hurt and surprised.)

LILY: I'm . . . I'm not making bad // choices
BLANCHE: Did you hear what I said, I don't want to get involved.
LILY: Why? I'm making bad choices—because—I'm having a *family?*

(Beat.)

BLANCHE: You're *sixteen.*
LILY: I'm *married.*
BLANCHE: Maybe that was a mistake?
LILY: My mother got married at my age. Was that a mistake?
BLANCHE: You're a teenager and you're married to a middle-aged man—and now you want to have *kids?* //
LILY *(Venom)*: I'm not a *lesbian* I can *have* them.

(Blanche grabs her book, switches off the lamp.)

(Suddenly stranded) Where are you going?
BLANCHE: Just don't throw your life on the rubbish heap alright?
LILY: I don't think *this* is a rubbish heap.
BLANCHE *(Gesturing to all the white stuff)*: Honey you live in an *igloo!*
LILY: So do *you.*
BLANCHE: Look: I'm grateful to have // this
LILY: Grateful means you keep your mouth *shut.*

(Beat.)

BLANCHE: No: *grateful* means you help someone who's helped you. *(Real feeling)* Now you helped me, didn't you, you got me this job. *(Beat)* And I need this job. I *need* this job. *(Beat)* So now I want to help you.

LILY *(Weakly)*: My family helps me.

BLANCHE: Your Family.

LILY: Ye.

BLANCHE: Is that what you believe?

LILY: Yes, they help me.

BLANCHE: Help you.

(She holds Lily's face in her hands.)

LILY *(Weaker)*: Yes.

BLANCHE: That's what you believe?

(Lily looks at Blanche; she's inexplicably and suddenly sad now. She nods yes weakly.)

LILY *(Holding back tears)*: Why? You think they . . . they don't *like* me?

[STOP]

(Blanche VERY SUDDENLY grabs Lily—tight. This is desperate, compulsive, out of measure—she's not in control of it.)

BLANCHE: Don't let these people decide your life for you, don't be a victim! *You* make the decision, *you* do it!

(Lily looks in her eyes, frightened and very curious.)

(Very, very vulnerable) You could make yourself a whole other person; it's right there Right in front of you . . . don't let them ruin // it

(Ike has entered down the stairs, wearing only pajama bottoms. He watches them, unseen.)

IKE *(To Lily)*: What are you doing?
LILY *(Startled)*: Oh. I //
IKE: Why are you still up.

(He notices she's been crying. He looks at Blanche—caught. Long pause.)

LILY: We were talking.
IKE: Come to bed.
LILY: Good night.
BLANCHE: And happy birthday.
LILY: Don't forget to. Uh. Pick up that stuff from—that cleaners.

(Blanche smiles a taut smile. Lily goes upstairs. Blanche stands there. Ike glowers at her—it's dreadfully uncomfortable. Eventually he turns around and walks upstairs. Blanche is left, solitary, still.)

8.

Shelly and JoJo's house.
They have Ike and Lily over for dinner.
They're eating pot roast with chopsticks.

SHELLY: The tap water's not koshah!

(Beat.)

IKE: Wha??
SHELLY: The rabbi said there's *crustaceans* //
IKE: in the *tap* // water?
SHELLY: *micro*-crustaceans //

JOJO: Lobsters—Crabs—*Micro* //

SHELLY *(To Lily)*: (Stop-playing-with-your-hands) //

JOJO: Only bottled water you // could drink

SHELLY *(To JoJo)*: You're not using your chopstick right.

JOJO: I'm using it // right.

SHELLY: You hold it between this finger and this finger not that // finger and this finger

JOJO: I'm holding it between this finger and // this finger

SHELLY: I said NOT that finger THIS finger.

[STOP]

(They eat in silence. Shelly monitors JoJo.)

How's the baby situation?

(Ike looks at Lily.)

LILY: (Adunknow.)

(They eat.)

JOJO: I'll tell you one thing, my kids are movin to Israel; they're moving to Israel and they're joining the freakin Israeli army.

(Lily looks at him, then goes back to playing with her food, lost in thought and feeling deeply out of place. A beat.)

IKE *(Bragging somewhat)*: You know what's not kosher?: snickers bars.

(They eat.)

SHELLY: Snickers and M&Ms.

(Ike darts a look to Shelly, scandalized.)

IKE: HEEE!

(*He covers his mouth.*)

JOJO: And twix!

(*Shelly looks over to JoJo dismissively.*)

SHELLY: Ca-an twix.

(*Shelly goes back to eating.*)

LILY: You want your *kid* to be in the *army*?
JOJO: What?
SHELLY: Israeli.
JOJO (*Hip-hop posturing*): Kill the palefreakin*stin*ians yo!

(*Beat. Lily just stares at him, disbelieving.*)

LILY: You're not even Israeli.

(*Ike puts down his fork, turns to her.*)

IKE: It's the Jewish *state*.
LILY: But we're Arabs.
SHELLY (*Makes a face*): We're not Arabs you gazzcase.

(*Beat.*)

LILY: Gramma speaks *Arabic*.
SHELLY: Ca-an she's a old lady.

(*Beat.*)

LILY: Well, would you kill your own relatives? Because that's //
what
JOJO: WE'RE NOT PALESTINIANS IDIOT—ah

LILY: We're Ara— //
SHELLY: They're *terrorists.*

(Beat.)

Finish your silvertip.

*(Shelly picks up her chopsticks and eats.
Pause.)*

LILY *(Quiet indignation)*: We're Arabs //
SHELLY: We're *Jews* dibeh, you know what Jewish is?
LILY: We have melanin in our skin. We come from the Ibe-
rian *Peninsula.*

(Beat.)

IKE: The *what*??
LILY: WE'RE SPANIARDS FROM THE IBERIAN PENIN-
SULA.

(Beat.)

IKE: Where are you learning this?
LILY: Don't you know your own *history*? that's who you *are.*
IKE *(Sarcasm)*: Oh, really, so who *am* I?

(Eyeballing her. A beat.)

LILY: There was an inquisition //
IKE: *Yeah*: and they murdered JEWS //
LILY: And then we moved to Syria and became Arabs //
JOJO: I //
IKE: Who's telling you this.

[STOP]

LILY (*Playing with her food*): We're not white //
IKE: Shut up.

(*Beat.*)

LILY: We're Iberian // people fr—
IKE (*Threat*): SHUT: UP.

(*They eat. Long silence.*)

JOJO (*To Shelly*): Did you get your passport?

(*Shelly doesn't answer.*)

IKE: I like the roast.
SHELLY: Silvertip.
JOJO (*His mouth full*): Tendah.

(*They eat.*)

LILY: What passport.
SHELLY (*To JoJo*): Don't play with that.
LILY: Where are you going?
SHELLY: China *dibeh.*
LILY: You're going?

(*She looks at Ike. He doesn't look at her.*)

SHELLY: I wanna try kung pao steak. //
JOJO: IT'S NOT KOSHER I TOLD YOU!
SHELLY: I wanna try certain restaurants, I wanna show you
    my fodors.
LILY (*To Shelly*): You're going to China?
SHELLY (*To JoJo*): Djousee my fodors?
JOJO: "Buddha's delight."

SHELLY: Oh I'm gonna miss my lessons at Padegat Could you tell Gerard? Oh and how's your backhand, is your wrist bettah?

LILY *(Trance)*: My . . .

(Pause.)

SHELLY: Your wrist?

IKE: Honey—

(Ike touches Lily's shoulder—she pushes him off and quickly exits.)

Whereyagoin?

(He goes after her.)

SHELLY *(To JoJo)*: And I want a Mao suit.

JOJO: Aright.

IKE: WHERE YA GOIN?

SHELLY: *You get bargains //*

JOJO: ARIGHT.

SHELLY *(To JoJo, pointing at her book)*: Look at my fodors, *I want that*!!

(Loud music.)

9.

Lily and Blanche.
Morning, a few days later, the living room.
Blanche is looking out of the window, cleaning. Lily sits back on the sofa, listless and out of sorts.

BLANCHE: Look at that cloud, it's like those cathedrals. I'd love to see those glistening white domes and minarets wouldn't you?

LILY: You want gum?

BLANCHE: Rome, Istanbul, I don't know I'd like to travel.

LILY: I thought you lived in Paris.

BLANCHE: I . . . I did.

LILY: So didn't you see em // then?

BLANCHE: I loved jogging the perimeter of the Jardin du Luxembourg and sometimes the Bois de Boulogne but I got shin splints cause the ground was unpaved it had rocks and things (oh, I miss bell) //

LILY: Who?

BLANCHE: hooks I told you about her She's a girl I'm friendly with she's like . . . well we were kind of close at one point.

LILY: Is she a philosopher?

BLANCHE: She doesn't believe in labels (Neither does my other friend Luce).

LILY: Who's //

BLANCHE: A feminist, this other girl I know from France? You seem out of sorts.

(Pause. Blanche peers out the window.)

LILY *(Glum)*: Did you get your teaching job?

BLANCHE: "I like a nice view but I like to sit with my back to it." That's a line from a book.

(Beat.
Blanche turns to see a rather enervated, depressed Lily.)

What's wrong?

LILY: Headache.

BLANCHE: When's your tennis lesson?

LILY: You know any songs in Spanish?

BLANCHE: You gotta find something to do, Lily. Otherwise you're gonna fester. "Lilies that fester smell far worse than weeds." That's Shakespeare.

(Blanche produces aspirin, water, hands them to Lily. Lily takes the aspirin and drinks the water down.)

LILY *(Plays with some taffy, stretches it out)*: Ikey's plane was delayed He called Something with the propellah.
BLANCHE: How long's he gonna be gone?
LILY: Two weeks, he went to China.
BLANCHE: Hip hip.
LILY *(Sad)*: He said not to come.
BLANCHE: Will the mice play?
LILY: Will you read to me?
BLANCHE *(Giving in)*: *Fine.*
LILY: Could I snuggle up on your lap?
BLANCHE: *No.*
LILY: *Please?*
BLANCHE: *Fine.*
LILY *(Vulgar command)*: Play with my haih!
BLANCHE *(Minstrelsy)*: Yes Miss Daisy //
LILY *(Holds up Blanche's purse)*: I like when you call me that. Zat your bag?
BLANCHE: Uh-huh.
LILY: Stunning-h.

(Lily pushes Blanche's hand onto her head, and uses her hand to play with her own hair—as if to train her—then looks up admiringly.)

BLANCHE *(Reads from Keats)*: "Ode on a Grecian Urn":
LILY: Ert.
BLANCHE: What "Ert"?

(More hand training. Blanche reads:)

> Thou still unravish'd bride of quietness,
>> Thou foster-child of Silence and slow Time,
> Sylvan historian, who canst thus express
>> A flowery tale more sweetly // than our rhyme:

LILY: You have nice cuticles.

BLANCHE: What? Uh—Oh—I bite them. *(Continues reading:)*
>> What men or gods are these? What maidens loth?
>> What mad pursuit? What struggle // to escape?

LILY *(Speaking over her)*: That's from nerves. Sometimes I bite the inside of my cheeks—is that weeid?

(Lily pulls a little talisman out of Blanche's purse.)

BLANCHE *(Continues reading)*:
>> What struggle to escape?
>>> What pipes and timbrels? What wild ecstasy? //

LILY *(Holds up talisman)*: whatsat? //

BLANCHE *(Grabs it, shoves it back in)*: *Stop goin through my things!* I thought you wanted me to read.

LILY: I do. What's this from?

BLANCHE: Keats.

LILY: It's boring.

BLANCHE: O *please //*

LILY: Poems and thing*s: ERT.*

BLANCHE: It's not *boring.*

LILY: It makes me tired.

BLANCHE: Is beauty boring?

LILY: Yes.

BLANCHE: Is *life //* boring?

LILY: I bought a new stunning belt with gold *pieces.*

(Exasperated pause.)

BLANCHE: You know what? You have to develop your aesthetics.

LILY *(Abstracted)*: Why?

BLANCHE: Cuz the apprehension of beauty is an essential part of being *human*, that's *why*. "Beauty is Truth, Truth Beauty."

LILY: I know: but beauty is *boring*—like I look at like a flower and I go: "Ye, petals, ca-an!"

BLANCHE: It's not just // petals!!

LILY: And plants—I *hate* them, I hate watering them, you get dirt all over the place from the water from when it leaks out and you track it on the *floah*!

(Blanche stares at her in disbelief.)

(Rifles through candy) Hee, I love gummy worms, I get naushus from them but-h. I like souah. *(Eats)* I like souah patch. I get naushus but-h.

(Blanche stares at her.)

What.

BLANCHE: Do you want me to read or not?

(Pause.)

What pipes and timbrels? What // wild

LILY: Could you clean behind the refrigerator?

BLANCHE *(Slams down her book)*: You have the *attention* span of an *aphid*.

LILY: Thehe's *mold*!

[STOP]

(Blanche bolts up to clean, picks up a rag.)

What's a aphid? //

BLANCHE: (Heard of a dictionary?)

LILY: Tickle my arm!

BLANCHE *(Throws down the rag)*: *I gotta go on break //*

LILY: The whole day is your break.

BLANCHE: Excuse you?!

LILY: You're lazy You don't do any work.

BLANCHE: Because you keep dragging me over to read you poems and play with your frizzy hair //

LILY: (I'm-using-hot-oil-treatments.)

BLANCHE: I just want to get *by*—Is that alright?

LILY: I thought you said you wanted to help me.

BLANCHE: I just want to get by: Is that *OK* with you? Can I get *by*?

[STOP]

LILY: You have an attitude problem.

BLANCHE *(Thrown)*: I have a *what*?

LILY *(Crossing her arms)*: It's not workin out—

BLANCHE: Don't you know that ALL black people have an attitude problem.

LILY *(Ingenuous)*: Yeah but why?

BLANCHE *(Minstrelsy)*: Well, you know dat just how we are! Druggies, welfare mothahs, dat's just how it is for us black folk—*we sho don't know any betta*!

LILY: You don't have to be so whiney about everything. Oprah doesn't whine.

BLANCHE: You need to be *slapped //*

LILY: You leave grime on the bath // tile!

BLANCHE: *Where's Ike Turner when you need //* him!

LILY: Pack your // things

BLANCHE: And your damn husband needs to take anger management classes.

LILY: He has *mood* swings and I *love* him for his mood swings! And you're a very nasty *girl //*

BLANCHE: Actually I'm not a GIRL.

LILY: I //

BLANCHE: And I'm not YOUR girl, I'm my own *woman* and I kicked and bit and screamed and ripped people apart to BE that so do not FUCK: WITH ME.

[STOP]

(Sorry-I-don't-know-what-came-over-me.)

(Lily is breathing rapidly, she's not well.)

Are. Are you—
LILY: Could you get my ativan.
BLANCHE: Are you alright?

(Lily slumps, dizzy, over to the sofa, covers her face, breathes heavy. Almost a whimpering. Blanche runs to Lily's purse, grabbing her ativan, gets her water, etc. Pause.)

I'm sorry. I didn't mean to //
LILY *(Looks up; she's terrified)*: I don't want to be alone.

(Beat.)

BLANCHE *(Smiling kindly)*: We're *all* alone sweetie.
LILY: I'm *not.*
BLANCHE: OK.
LILY: I'm not alone.

(Beat.)

BLANCHE: You can rest your head on my lap.

*(Lily does.
Beat.)*

LILY: Will you tickle my arm?

(Blanche tickles her arm.)

You're not really fired *Anna Maria.*

(Blanche smiles. She plays with Lily's hair for a while.)

BLANCHE: Takin the pills?

(Lily nods.)

And you popped em out and put em in the midol bottle like I said?

LILY: Ye.

BLANCHE: Can't miss a day, even when he's gone, OK?

(Lily looks up at her lovingly.)

LILY: Thank you. Blanche.

BLANCHE *(Smiles)*: What'd you call me?

LILY: You have such a nice face.

BLANCHE *(Laughs; a little shy)*: Oh, please.

LILY: You do, you have good bone structure.

BLANCHE *(Giggles awkwardly)*: Uhhh . . . whatever.

LILY: You have high cheekbones.

BLANCHE: Thanks.

LILY: Does that prevent you from sleeping in certain positions?

(Blanche looks at Lily, laughs. The laughter subsides. Pause.)

BLANCHE *(Surprisingly flirtatious)*: I'm adept at many positions.

(Lily has no idea what that means but knows it's some kind of pick-up line. Blanche snaps out of it, sits up.)

(Panicked—defusing) Uh. Oh—Oh You-know-who-has-good-bone-structure? Iman.

[STOP]

(Lily instinctively leans in and kisses Blanche. Blanche leans in for a second, then pushes her off, stands.)

(Smiling awkwardly) Oh, OK, no thank you. Uh—

(Lily, like a magnet, springs up and is on her, glued to her face. Blanche tries to speak, her voice muffled by the kiss. She works to push Lily off. This doesn't work, not even a little.)

Act Two

The Pleasure of the Text

1.

Blanche and Lily.
Blanche's room.
Music playing softly in the background, maybe something 1980s.
They're tasting wines. There's a bunch of wine bottles out—
they're both slightly tipsy.
Their intimacy is significantly evolved here.

BLANCHE: Swish.

    (Lily swishes.)

Through the teeth. Slurp.

    (Lily gargles.)

It's not listerine, honey. Watch: *comme ça.*

(Blanche slurps.
Lily slurps.)

What do you feel?

LILY: Firmness?

BLANCHE: Are you asking me or telling me.

LILY: Aduknow!

BLANCHE: Feel it evaporate in your retronasal passage //

LILY *(Wine in mouth)*: OK //

BLANCHE: (No swallow first.)

LILY: I taste . . . burnt match?

BLANCHE: Good //

LILY: (And grass?)

BLANCHE: What else?

LILY: Can we just drink?

BLANCHE: You don't want to get too drunk.

LILY: I do.

BLANCHE: The French don't drink too get drunk //

LILY: (I'm Jewish) *What's this?*

BLANCHE: Châteauneuf du Pape.

LILY: S'it good?

BLANCHE: 1950 that's a great year This is an excellent vineyard—

LILY: It is?

BLANCHE: Microclimatic Small yields No this is *incroyable* ooh grrrrrrl (here sniff).

(She does.)

LILY: It's . . . cheeky.

BLANCHE *(Laughing)*: What's that mean?

LILY: I don't know.

BLANCHE: You're cheeky.

(A whiff of sexual tension; Blanche pulls back.)

That's a '99 Leroy.

LILY: Shoof.

BLANCHE: They're one of the great producers of white bur-
gundy //

(She sniffs.)

LILY: You know so much //

BLANCHE: (Oak on the nose) I make it my business to know.
If you make something your business, you know it inside
out.

LILY: I know you inside out.

(Beat.)

BLANCHE *(Cynical laughter)*: That's what you think.

LILY *(Playfully brazen)*: That's what I *know*.

(Pause.)

BLANCHE: Don't you know it's dangerous to trust people you
don't know very well.

LILY: I feel light.

(Pause.)

BLANCHE: You want something to hold on to, that's all. You
haven't found yourself, that's why. You don't know who
you are, you haven't found yourself.

LILY *(Drunken flirting)*: Who am I?

(She gets close to her face.)

Who am I?

(She kisses her; Blanche pulls away.)

What.

BLANCHE: Nothing; you remind me of someone.
LILY: Did she love you?

(Pause.)

BLANCHE: Not like that.

(Pause.)

LILY: Because *I* love you.

[STOP]

BLANCHE: *No.*
LILY *(Almost weeping)*: I *love* you //
BLANCHE: You—ha ha. Y—you're just a tadpole //
LILY: I'm not a tadpole!
BLANCHE *(Shooing)*: Swim away little fishie you're too young.
LILY: But //
BLANCHE: (Go find a nice Syrian girl // and)
LILY: NO.
BLANCHE: I am *forty-three.*
LILY: So?
BLANCHE: So I'm not going to take advantage of a sixteen-//-year-old girl.
LILY: (Seventeen) you're not taking // advant—
BLANCHE *(Resisting)*: It's not *ethical* //
LILY: I know you like me.
BLANCHE: Once is OK, but that's it; I'm not embroiling you in this.
LILY: In *what?*

(Beat.)

What about Adrienne Rich //
BLANCHE: She's passé.

(Beat.)

LILY *(Assured)*: I think you're in love with me.

(A shift.)

BLANCHE: When's hubby comin back?
LILY: He's in the Orient.
BLANCHE: I know *that* but // when's he
LILY: A few days.

(Pause.)

BLANCHE: Let's just sit here with our little fluted glasses and chop it up alright?
LILY: Chop what up?
BLANCHE: Talk.

(Blanche downs a glass of wine, pours herself another.)

LILY: Where'd you grow up?
BLANCHE: Moved around.
LILY: No but—when you were adopted.
BLANCHE: I was twelve.
LILY: And // you
BLANCHE: And I moved to Philadelphia //
LILY: Liberty bell? //
BLANCHE: With the crack, yeah //
LILY: And then you lived in the homeless shelter?
BLANCHE *(Regretting telling her this)*: That was later.

(Beat.)

LILY *(Bright)*: I never met anyone from a homeless shelter!!
BLANCHE *(Dry)*: Yeah, tick it off.

(She downs some wine.)

LILY: And were your parents nice? What were they like?

BLANCHE *(Frozen smile)*: I don't want to talk about him.

LILY: Who?

BLANCHE: I mean *them.*

LILY: Why?

(Pause.)

BLANCHE: Cuz it's the past It's an illusion.

(Beat.)

LILY: But you said you have to know the past.

BLANCHE: Yeah but //

LILY: You said if you don't know history you become its victim—you're contradicting yourself.

BLANCHE: "I'm not contradictory: I am *dispersed*": Roland Barthes.

LILY: Ooh I got a flash card fa him //

BLANCHE: Keep up the flash cards.

(Beat.)

LILY *(Naifish curiosity)*: What were their names?

BLANCHE: Who?

LILY: Your parents?

(Beat. Then wearily:)

BLANCHE *(Sighing)*: Rich and Audrey.

LILY: "Rich and Audrey" //

BLANCHE: White //

LILY: "Audrey White" that's a pretty name //

BLANCHE: No: *They* were *white.*

LILY: Were they nice?

(Beat. Blanche doesn't look at her.)

BLANCHE: Will you stop *asking* // me that?

LILY: I'm // curious

BLANCHE *(Snaps at her)*: NO they weren't nice they were fucking *horrible* is that what you want to hear?! Fingers on me middle a the night in my room night after night Think anyone did a goddamn thing to stop it? "You're *black* You're a *woman* You're at the bottom of the *world.*" Know how many times I heard that shit?!

(Lily takes a sip of wine, discomfited. Long awkward pause.)

(Forcing a tiny smile) So—so did you. Didja ever think about—*girls* before?

LILY *(Softening)*: Not before this.

BLANCHE: Not even *once?*

(Beat.)

LILY: Well once.

[STOP]

BLANCHE: OK-wait-let-me-get-comfortable //

LILY: When I was in the dressing room //

BLANCHE: Where //

LILY: Loehmann's //

BLANCHE *(Blunt)*: What's *Loehmann's* //

LILY: (You get bras and coats) //

BLANCHE: Oh.

LILY: There's a public dressing room //

BLANCHE *(Swirling her wine)*: They say a public dressing room is a dyke's business office //

LILY: (Really?) //

BLANCHE: (No.)

LILY: So my mother used to take // me

BLANCHE: Loooooehmann's //

LILY: And I was really young, and I saw—you know; "that stuff."

(*Beat.*)

BLANCHE: *"Stuff"?*
LILY: That. Yeah.
BLANCHE (*Amused*): And you liked it.
LILY: Aduknow.
BLANCHE: Well *did* you or *didn't* you?

(*Beat.*)

LILY: I wasn't aware that I liked it? But . . . I think looking back? . . . Ye. //
BLANCHE (*Mock warning*): *But don't look back //*
LILY: *What?*
BLANCHE (*Smiling at her inside joke*): Pillar of salt, etceteras—
LILY: Oh.
BLANCHE: But we'll *all* go to hell now WHEEEEEE //
LILY: I don't feel good //
BLANCHE: (It could be the sulfites Are you asthmatic?) //
LILY: I feel like I could fall.
BLANCHE: You're just drunk.
LILY: You're not.
BLANCHE: I drink all the time, It's the law of diminishing returns //
LILY: Could you play with my haih?
BLANCHE (*Drinks*): (Needs more of a backbone) //
LILY: Tickle my arm.

(*Blanche demurs at first, but eventually does, she grazes Lily's arm lightly with her fingernails. There's real longing. Lily starts looking through Blanche's purse.*)

You have mints?
BLANCHE: I don't think so.

LILY (*Pulls something out from her purse*): Whassis?
BLANCHE: A pad *Don't look through my stuff.*

(*Lily pulls out a gun and sits up, alarmed.*)

LILY: *What's that?*
BLANCHE: *Gimme that.*

(*Blanche grabs the gun away from Lily.*)

Girl's gotta protect herself.

(*Blanche shoves the gun back in her purse, moves the purse away from Lily. Lily settles back into Blanche's lap.*)

LILY: I'm drunk. I want a mint-h!

(*Blanche goes back to grazing Lily's arm.*)

(*Relaxing a bit*) I want a mint.

(*Blanche looks at her, strokes her arm. It's love.*)

BLANCHE: So were you in love at first sight?
LILY: With who?
BLANCHE: Hubby.
LILY: I was twelve. He used to buy me gum.
BLANCHE: Didn't the age difference bother your parents?
LILY: My father is much older than my mother.
BLANCHE: Where'd you meet?
LILY: My cousin's wedding, Julie, she drives a mitsubishi galant.
BLANCHE: That's nice.
LILY: (I like jaguars) //
BLANCHE (*A bit of self-torture*): And you started dating?
LILY: He took me for ice cream.
BLANCHE (*Curled irony*): And did you get all *excited* when you'd see him?

LILY: Aduknow.

BLANCHE *(Playful mocking)*: Did you think, like, "*Oooh Prailines and Cream!*"?

LILY *(Scrunched face)*: It was more I was nervous; my stomach hurt. I think I was excited, I was pretty young. I'm more matured now. Then I was a baby. Sometimes I would feel sick.

BLANCHE: A good sick?

LILY *(Guileless, a bit more drunk)*: Well I'd throw up. But I'm more matured now; I don't throw up anymore; I got a lot of stomach viruses; my mother told me I had a sensitive stomach.

BLANCHE: And how did he propose?

(Lily is lost in thought. There's a shift into melancholy.)

How did he propose // to

LILY: But I don't think it's right when people trick people.

BLANCHE: You // what—

LILY: I don't like that It's not right.

BLANCHE: Who tricked you?

LILY *(Drunk)*: NO I didn't say that, you don't listen: What I said was I don't think it's RIGHT to trick someone.

(Blanche backs off. She takes a sip of wine.)

When did you first . . . have . . . like . . . sex or whatever.

BLANCHE *(Lying)*: I can't remember.

LILY: How could you not remember. How old // were

BLANCHE: *I can't remember.*

[STOP]

LILY: Did. Did people tell you . . . what it was?

BLANCHE *(A dark undercurrent)*: I kinda happened upon it.

(Pause.)

LILY: I thought it was if you touched someone a certain way. Or. If someone *touched* you? *(Pause)* I was ignorant.

(Blanche looks at her.)

BLANCHE: No one talked about it to you?

LILY: And he said I wasn't a *virgin* anymore? So then I said that I *would* marry him. Because . . . my reputation would be ruined.

(Pause.)

(Tearing up) But then I *was* a virgin . . .

(Blanche's expression slowly turns steely. Long pause.)

BLANCHE: And you never said anything?

LILY *(Still shaken)*: My reputation would // be

BLANCHE *(Punishing)*: So you're a victim.

LILY: No . . . I //

BLANCHE: Yeah you are.

LILY: I'm not a //

BLANCHE: You think cuz you ain't equipped to handle life you ain't accountable?

[STOP]

You think people are gonna feel sorry for you? "Oh poor baby, no one raised her, no one gave a shit, so now *we* gotta help her?"—because *nobody* cares if you lose, the world's full a losers! Losers get *punished* for being losers, nobody fucking cares—it's the *winners* people care about! You gotta rip yourself up and start // over—!

(Lily shudders, jerks her head to the left, sharp intake of breath—it's the "ghost.")

LILY: It's here—
BLANCHE: What?
LILY *(Panic)*: That—it's—It's in here The—I just saw it again.
BLANCHE: Where?

(Lily is still, alert; her eyes dart nervously. Blanche looks at Lily, gets increasingly spooked. She looks out, sensing a presence in the room. Her breathing gets unsteady. The silence is fraught with terror; they're both too frightened to move. It goes on like this for a bit.
Lily tentatively relaxes her posture a little bit.)

LILY: I . . . I think it's gone now.

(She approaches Blanche from behind, touches her lightly on the shoulder. Blanche gasps, shudders, jerks her head.)

It's only me.

(Blanche turns to see her.)

BLANCHE *(Denial)*: I don't believe in ghosts.

(She turns away from her; ineptly tries to make light of it.)

You givin me the creeps.
LILY *(Hurt)*: But . . . I . . . I *saw* it.

(Beat.)

BLANCHE *(Feigned indifference)*: They can't haunt you if you don't acknowledge em; pretend it's not there.

(Lily looks at her, not quite comforted by this.)

LILY: Will you sleep with me tonight?

(Blanche hesitates. Eventually she nods yes.)

We can sleep here in your room. I don't like to be alone.
BLANCHE *(Throws her a t-shirt)*: Sleep in this.

(They get dressed for bed. Lily's having some trouble with the t-shirt.)

LILY: I don't like it when you yell at me.
BLANCHE: I didn't yell at you.
LILY *(Drunk)*: You did, you said "I'M AT THE BOTTOM OF THA EARTH I'M BLACK."
BLANCHE: (Sorry) //
LILY: I don't like that I get scahed.
BLANCHE: I'm just worried about stuff; it's not you. I have a lot of. Uh—things on my mind.
LILY *(A caper)*: Like what-h? maybe I could help!
BLANCHE *(Lying)*: My. My—loans and stuff are due.
LILY: From college?
BLANCHE: I used up my deferments they said. They're coming after me.
LILY: But we're paying you
BLANCHE: Yeah enough for food and c'est tout. *(Bright)* I'll be OK—I'm just
LILY: You'll pay them back.
BLANCHE *(Forcing a smile)*: I'll get a teaching job soon enough.

(Pause.)

LILY: Well. I have this checkbook—why don't I write you one.
BLANCHE: One what?
LILY: *Check* dibeh!

(Beat.)

BLANCHE: *No.*
LILY: I *want* to.
BLANCHE: It's not your responsibility.
LILY *(Sincere, lovingly)*: *You're* my responsibility.

(Long pause.)

BLANCHE *(Moved, despite herself)*: You don't even *know* me.
LILY: He said I should write you checks, how much is it for?

(Lily opens her purse and pulls out her checkbook.)

BLANCHE: You're crazy, I'm not taking *money* from you!
LILY: You helped me; now let me help you.

*(Blanche looks at her.
Lily fills out and signs a check.)*

(Girlish) Look Don't I forge his signature good?

*(Lily hands the check to her. Blanche looks at it. Slowly
she takes it, looks down at it. It's real. She laughs. She looks
at Lily and shakes her head. She looks down at the check
again. She begins to weep—the tears come from a deep,
deep, wounded place.)*

BLANCHE: That's eight thousand dollars.
LILY *(Bright)*: Now you can stay!
BLANCHE: I can't take this from you!
LILY: Yes you can.

(Pause.)

BLANCHE *(Embarrassed laughter)*: *Gracias* Lily.
LILY: *De nada.*
BLANCHE: *Ojalá no se enoje.*
LILY: *El no se enterará.*

BLANCHE *(Laughs)*: I hope you're right.

> *(Lily kisses Blanche on the cheek, a quick peck. Lily fluffs a pillow. Blanche gets under the covers.)*

LILY: Let's go to bed I got a tennis lesson in the morning—
BLANCHE: I got laundry.

> *(Snap blackout.)*

2.

Five days later, morning. The living room.
Blanche is repainting the minimalist walls. Ike's back from China, doing the crossword. He's wearing a suit; he looks especially groomed. He is wound up and angry.
Lily enters, she's on cloud nine, a woman in love.

LILY: I finished unpacking your stuff.
IKE: What?
LILY: Welcome back!

> *(Ike continues with his crossword, not looking at her. Lily looks at him, cheery.)*

IKE: Stop looking at me.
LILY: What?
IKE *(Not looking up)*: You keep lookin at me funny.
LILY: You look nice. You never wear suits to work.
IKE *(Weirdly uncomfortable)*: I got a meeting.
LILY: With Jo?

> *(Beat.)*

IKE: I gotta meet with some people.

(Beat.)

LILY: So how was it? did you see the wall?
IKE: That's Germany //
LILY: *Yeah* and also CHINA.

(Beat.)

I like that suit // on you
IKE *(Fillip of hostility)*: WILL YOU SHUT UP ABOUT MY
SUIT, I CAN WEAR A SUIT IF I WANNA WEAR A
SUIT!

(Lily looks at him, smiling indifferently.)

LILY *(Irony)*: Sexy when you get mad.

*(Ike knows he's insulted her but can't figure out how.
Blanche smiles to herself and continues to paint. Lily picks
up a book: Barthes's S/Z. She reads.)*

IKE: Hear any news? //
LILY *(Terse, not looking up)*: I'm not pregnant.

(Beat.)

IKE: You spoke to the // doctor?
LILY *(Perfunctory)*: There's nothing wrong with me //
IKE: Well there's nothing wrong with *me*.

(She reads. Ike glowers at her.)

Did you hear what I said //
LILY: "There's nothing wrong with me."
IKE *(Turns to face her)*: Where were you last night?
LILY: Here.

IKE: I woke up you were gone.

LILY: I couldn't sleep.

BLANCHE *(Repainting, cheery)*: We're running outta "snowball."

LILY *(Gets up to exit)*: I'll get more.

IKE: Let the G get it.

*(A little flirtatious pantomime behind Ike's back:
Lily winks seductively at Blanche.
Blanche smiles flirtatiously and licks her lips.
Ike, sensing something, turns his head; Blanche instantly re-
sumes her default painting position; Lily tries to act casual.)*

LILY: What—

IKE: Why don't you—

*(Ike cuts off mid-sentence. They resume flirting. He quickly
shifts back around, eyeballs them.)*

LILY *(Caught)*: I'm not doing anything—

IKE: *What was that?*

LILY *(Innocently)*: *What?*

*(Ike slowly pivots back and resumes the crossword.
Blanche giggles to herself. Lily pretends to be interested in
Ike. Blanche flashes her tit as Lily exits. Lily tries to stifle
her laughter.
Ike, sensing something, shifts abruptly to look at her and
Blanche—who narrowly escapes exposure. He's getting
angry.)*

IKE *(Punishing her)*: Get me cream.

BLANCHE: It's on the table.

IKE: It's not on the table.

*(Blanche walks over and takes the cream, which is three
inches away from him, and positions it two inches from*

him—then flashes her best "innocent helper" smile. She goes back to painting.
Ike gets up to feed the goldfish.)

(To Kitty) Hiiiiiiiiiiiiiieeeeeeeeee. Hiiii honey!! Awwwwwwwwwww.

(Blanche looks over at him. She rolls her eyes. He senses her looking at him and quickly jerks his head to catch her. She deftly resumes painting. He sidles over to her. He leans against the wall, almost hovering. Blanche continues to paint.)

Nice bracelets.
BLANCHE: What, oh these Oh they're bangles.
IKE: Very sharp, where'd you get em?
BLANCHE *(Lying)*: The mall.

(She continues to paint.)

IKE *(To Blanche)*: You didn't by any chance mention anything to anyone did you?
BLANCHE: Bout what?
IKE: When you were in my office . . . ? you didn't happen to see anything?
BLANCHE: When I was cleaning?
IKE: Mention anything?

[STOP]

You wouldn't screw me would you?

(Blanche looks him up and down.)

BLANCHE *(Dryly)*: I wouldn't.
IKE: Did you open your big mouth?

(Blanche notices that half his suit is covered in white paint.)

You look nervous.
BLANCHE: I. Your suit—
IKE *(Facetious)*: What I don't MATCH?
BLANCHE: No—you—

(Ike realizes he has paint on his suit.
Lily enters holding a paint can.)

LILY: I can't find the— (HEEE.)
IKE *(Points at Blanche)*: Why does she have to do that?
LILY *(Recites dutifully)*: It's minimalism.
IKE: You think it's funny?
LILY: The decorator // said
IKE *(Upset)*: IT'S NOT FUNNY.
LILY: I don't think it's funny!

(Ike exits.)

(Calls after him) I-don't-think-it's—

(She and Blanche lock eyes. They laugh and laugh mis-
chievously, but there's real intimacy.
The laughing grows uncontrollable, hysterical. Eventu-
ally it is drowned out by the sound of a woman speaking
French—a language lesson CD.)

3.

Bedroom, night.
Ike is going over receipts, Lily is practicing French. The CD
overlaps their conversation.

TAPE: I am hungry: *"J'ai faim."*

LILY: *"J'ai faim."*
TAPE: I am thirsty: *"J'ai soif."*
LILY: *"J'ai soif."*
TAPE: I am frightened: *"J'ai peur."*
IKE: I'm missing // money.
LILY: *"J'ai peur."*
TAPE: I am cold: *"J'ai fois."*
LILY: *"J'ai"* //
IKE: I'm *missing money.*
TAPE: I am hot: *"J'ai chaud."*

(*Beat.*)   .

LILY: From where?
IKE: The *bank.*
LILY: You gave // me a checkbook.
TAPE: I am afraid to take the plane: *"J'ai peur de prendre l'avion."*
IKE: You spent eight *grand* in one shot?
LILY: *"J'ai peur de prendre l'avion."*

(*Ike slams the CD off.*)

IKE: Whaddayou spending eightthousanddollars for.

(*Pause.*)

LILY: I needed it.
IKE: For what
LILY: I don't have to tell you.
IKE: THAT'S MY MONEY

(*Short pause.*)

LILY: What's yours is mine Right? Isn't that what a marriage
is? I take what I want from you and you take what you
want // from me.

IKE: Why are you acting this way.

LILY: Because you're a liar.

IKE: How am I a liar?

(She turns to him.)

LILY: Because I talked to my sister and she told me you stole money from Jo and that they fired you last week. And that's why you're wearing a suit and screaming at me because you keep lying to me. Because you can't bribe me with money because we don't have any money. And no one's gonna hire you because everyone knows you're a thief.

(Pause.)

IKE: That's bullshit.

LILY: You *knew* she'd tell me.

(Beat.)

IKE: I didn't steal money. I. I re-allocated it.

LILY: Yeah.

(She turns the CD on again; he slams it right off.)

IKE: And don't you fucking tell me off. I won't be spoken to by my own wife like this and I'm—HEY. *(Grabs her)* I'm having a rough week, I don't need to come home to you calling me names.

(Silence.)

And there are plenny a people who'd kill to work with me so shut your mouth You don't know what you're talking about. You hear me? I know how to run a *business* That's why you live good because I know what I'm doin.

LILY: Like your father, like how he ran a business?

IKE *(Hoarsely)*: *Don't talk about him.*

LILY: My sister // said

IKE: You're sister's a fucking liar, alright?

LILY: No, you're a liar. You.

(Pause.)

(Quiet and so sad) You tricked me . . .

[STOP]

(He kisses her hair. She's momentarily helpless—he's got power over her.)

IKE: I'm gonna take care of you.

LILY: Stop it //

IKE: I'm gonna take care of you . . . daddy's gonna take care of his baby OK?

(Lily, in a single gesture, disentangles herself. She opens a drawer and grabs a bottle of expensive wine.)

What's that?

(She grabs a corkscrew and opens it expertly.)

LILY: Keeps the cork intact //

IKE: You don't *drink* //

LILY: I do now, *Pouilly-Fumé*, medium-bodied white //

IKE: Since when do you drink?

LILY: I started a wine cellar.

IKE: IN YOUR DRAW?

LILY: Anna Maria taught me about *tasting* //

IKE: *Who?!*

LILY *(Squinting)*: She's an oenophile.

(She swishes; slurps some wine. He looks at her.)

IKE: *I don't want you drinking wine //*
LILY *(Swirling)*: Honey, cantaloupe //
IKE: You're not old enough // to
LILY: Oh I'm not *old* enough? *Really?* Talk more about that.

(Long pause.)

I think we should. Get an annulment.
IKE: What?

(Pause.
She turns, looks right at him.)

(Terrified) Who's putting ideas in your head?
LILY: I have my *own* ideas.
IKE: Is it that *nigger?*

(She looks at him, enraged.)

[STOP]

Where's my money?
LILY: You are an ignorant. Old. Man //

(Ike grabs the glass of wine as she's about to drink it and throws it in her face.)

IKE *(Leaning in)*: And you're turning into a spoiled little *brat* I don't like it.

(He does pushups. She's brewing.)

Fifteen. Sixteen.

(She starts attacking him, hitting him. It barely affects him. She kicks him, etc., but she's slight. He waits until she's out of breath. She's miserable, frustrated, humiliated, angry. He's impassive and his impassivity makes her angrier.)

Seventeen. *Don't do that again.*

(Pause.)

Eighteen. Nineteen. Twenty (I'm warning you.)

(Lily attacks him. Blanche enters with the laundry.)

BLANCHE *(Smiling obliviously)*: I forgot the whites //

(Ike bolts up.)

IKE: WHADAISAY?

(Lily eyeballs him; quiet and confident.)

LILY: You don't have power over me.

[STOP]

*(He smacks her across the face.
She smacks him right back.)*

[STOP]

*(In a single move, he punches Lily square in the face. Blanche is terrified, paralyzed.
In the next section they speak quickly over each other, it's a bit chaotic.)*

IKE: Do NOT touch my person do you hear me, you don't EVER touch me, EVER, do you hear // me

BLANCHE: I //

IKE: And YOU you just bought a ticket to your own funeral *did you // hear me.*

LILY *(Cups her hand over her eye)*: You // hit me

IKE *(To Blanche)*: You're DEAD, did // you hear me.

BLANCHE: Who // me

LILY: *¿Me lastimó, // viste lo que hizo?*

BLANCHE: *¿Estás // bien?*

IKE: WHAT DID // YOU SAY TO HER?

LILY: *Tengo que irme de aquí; promete que nos iremos.*

BLANCHE: I promise //

IKE: WHAT DID // SHE SAY TO YOU??

LILY *(Still stunned)*: You hit // me.

IKE *(Shame. Then to Blanche)*: Good-bye, back in your // cage.

BLANCHE: I //

LILY: (You // hit me.)

IKE: Get // *out!*

BLANCHE: Lily //

IKE: GET OUT!!

(Snap blackout.)

4.

Sounds of tennis balls being lobbed about.
The lounge area of an indoor tennis court.
Lily and Shelly in tennis outfits, headbands, sweaty. Lily is twirling her racquet.
She has a black eye.

SHELLY: The silks were nice. We saw a silkworm farm. A place where they make silkworms. *(Beat)* I mean not silkworms I mean, HA HA, where the silkworms are. Where they *make silk. (Beat)* I was gagging from the smell. ERT.

LILY: Does it smell?

SHELLY: (The silk is nice but-h.)
LILY: My backhand's improving Gerard said.
SHELLY: My knee hurts.

(A pause as Lily adjusts a string on her racquet.)

LILY: So, how are you feeling?
SHELLY: When I was carrying Ricky I was bad, when I had
    Joey—*Stevie*—but // aduknow
LILY: Do you want something else to drink?
SHELLY: I wish they had sprite; I don't like this OTHAH
    CRAP-ah.

(Beat.)

LILY: Do you know anything about Chicago? //
SHELLY: Windy. //
LILY: You were never theh? //
SHELLY *(Picks up glass)*: Wisconsin, Ohio, aduknow. *(Sips)*
    *You know who's theh—Oprah. (Sips, then pushes glass
    away with histrionic disgust)* ERT I'm NAUSHUS. You
    want my lemon?

*(Pause.
The sounds of tennis balls being lobbed.)*

You need to be pregnant.
LILY: Yeah.
SHELLY: "Yeah."

(Beat.)

What's with you?

(Pause.)

LILY: I'm getting an annulment.

(Shelly laughs at her.)

It's not funny.

SHELLY *(Dismissing)*: Oh please. The string on my racquet broke look at this—

LILY: He stole money.

SHELLY: We'll get the money back.

LILY *(After a beat)*: He *lied.*

SHELLY: You're not getting an *annulment.*

LILY: I'm bisexual. I was talking to Blanche that's what she said.

(Lily sucks on the lemon wedge innocuously.)

SHELLY: What's what who said?

LILY: I'm not a lesbian.

SHELLY: Who's *Blanche?*

LILY: My maid.

SHELLY: Why is your *maid* telling you you're a bisexual?

(Pause.)

LILY *(Regretting telling her)*: Tell me more about the silk farm.

SHELLY: Is your *maid* a bisexual?

LILY *(Sucking the lemon)*: Lesbian.

SHELLY: *Back up //*

LILY: You want gum?

SHELLY: NO I DON'T WANT GUM.

(Pause.)

LILY: I'm moving to Chicago.

SHELLY *(Laughing)*: With who your *maid?*

LILY: She has tenure track

SHELLY *(Giddy)*: *Op*-stay already I *caaan't.*

LILY: Northwestern. It's the ivy league.

[STOP]

(Shelly is speechless.)

She has connections //
SHELLY: What is she gonna teach toilet scrubbing?
LILY: Semiotics //
SHELLY: OK: *you're not a lesbian* //
LILY: Which is //
SHELLY: I-DON'T-WANT-TO-KNOW-WHAT-IT-IS.
LILY: She has a PhD.
SHELLY: Yeah she's a freakin genius.
LILY: She quotes poetry do you?
SHELLY: No I don't quote POETRY Lilian I'm too busy clean-
    ing up my kids' VOMIT. *(Pause)* I gotta go to my jeweler
    It's almost six—
LILY: Wait //
SHELLY: You smell: go shower.
LILY *(Very tender)*: I love someone; I never had that before.

(Shelly scrutinizes her like meat.)

SHELLY: *Shame on you.*

[STOP]

(She gets up to leave. Lily grabs her arm.)

LILY: Shel //
SHELLY: *I thought you wanted kids.*

(Beat.)

LILY: I'm on the pill.
SHELLY: You're *what?* I thought //
LILY: Don't tell him.

*(A recognition of Lily's duplicity slowly registers on
Shelly's face.)*

SHELLY: I have to go //

LILY: Please // don't

SHELLY: No I don't want to hear this *shit.*

LILY *(Heartbroken)*: *Why?*

SHELLY: Why, because it's making me SICK. *(Beat)* I'm *pregnant* and you're making me *sick.*

LILY: I //

SHELLY: I was doing you a *favor.* You think JoJo wanted to go into business with your low-life husband—*that was from me*! *(Beat)* And then you spit in my *face?*

LILY: I'm sorry.

SHELLY: *Pig.*

(Pause.)

LILY: I appreciate everything you // and

SHELLY *(Shaking her head; to herself)*: No I don't *want* your appreciation Don't *waste it on me.*

(Lily zips up her tennis racquet in its case.)

LILY: I thought we could be . . . *close.* I

SHELLY *(Looks at her—steely)*: You're. Committing. Suicide.

LILY *(Feigning bravery)*: People can think what they want //

SHELLY: You're not a *fucking* lesbian //

LILY *(Quiet tears, but trying to stay composed)*: I'm //

SHELLY: And we'll see how you don't care what people think, we'll see. And don't you DARE come crawling to me on your hands and knees because I'll kick you right in the throat. You'll get *nothing.*

LILY *(Stunned)*: Don't talk to me like that.

SHELLY: How should I talk to you? What do you feel you *deserve?* you feel proud of yourself?

LILY: I—I thought I could come to you.

SHELLY: *Why?* You think you can bring your filthy news to me? Do you have such a *low* opinion of me?

(Silence.)

LILY *(A plea)*: But. I'm. I'm . . . not *happy.*
SHELLY: *So be unhappy.*
LILY: Like you?
SHELLY: That's right. Like me You're damn *right* like me—

(Lily exits.)

I feel sorry for your husband.

5.

Blanche and Lily.
The living room, daytime.
Blanche is dustbusting. Lily is eating candies and little confec-
tions and chatting excitedly.

LILY: And there were peonies and hydrangeas // and
BLANCHE: And were they just *petals*?
LILY: No.
BLANCHE: See?

(Blanche gives her a peck on the cheek.)

LILY: And I became a member of Channel 13!

(Lily produces a tote/duffel bag with the PBS logo
emblazoned.)

BLANCHE: Nice //
LILY: (And-also-they-gave-me-a-comb) //
BLANCHE: Did you make your // flash cards?
LILY: And there was a flower shaped like—oh what's it called?
    (Snap, snap) OOLIE.
BLANCHE: A forsythia?

LILY: No.

BLANCHE: A daisy?

LILY: A *hyacinth.*

BLANCHE: Oh "the hyacinth girl."

LILY: What?

BLANCHE: What? Oh that's // from

LILY: Yeah a flower.

BLANCHE: Shaped like a hyacinth?

LILY: No.

BLANCHE *(Dustbusting under her feet)*: (Lift.)

LILY *(Lifting her feet up)*: No it was—insects—it was like in-
    sects, like these. Uh. *Bright* insects, and they were green,
    and they would form themselves like that, it was very
    mysterious

BLANCHE: To escape predators.

LILY: YES.

BLANCHE: It's not mysterious it's nature survival of the species.

LILY: Oh.

(Beat.)

BLANCHE: (Down) How's your eye?

LILY *(Putting her feet down)*: Better //

BLANCHE: Where's Rich?

LILY: What?

BLANCHE: I mean—hubby.

LILY: Aduknow he stays out late.

BLANCHE: He's watching me. I keep thinking he's gonna turn
    a corner and appear outta nowhere He scares me.

LILY: He thinks you got him fired.

BLANCHE *(Laughs, exasperated)*: I was there *one* day.

LILY: Where?

BLANCHE: His *office*, I'm not *that* good at bookkeeping!

LILY: He's paranoid.

(Beat.)

BLANCHE: You goin to your sister's?

(Lily doesn't respond, a shift.)

LILY: I'm not talking to her.
BLANCHE: Why?
LILY: No reason.
BLANCHE: She loves you.
LILY: She doesn't like *you.*
BLANCHE *(Chipper)*: Cause I'm black and she's racist it's perfectly consistent.
LILY: She said the n word.
BLANCHE: I heard, I don't mind. It's just a signifier—and what are signifiers?
LILY: Arbitrary //
BLANCHE: And what is all language?
LILY: Metaphor.
BLANCHE: Because //
LILY: There's no relationship between things and words //
BLANCHE: "Necessary" //
LILY: (Necessary) but you keep telling me that she *doesn't* love me.
BLANCHE: Well—her love is *degraded* but she has good intentions.

(Beat.)

LILY: She said I was a pig.
BLANCHE: Why would she say that?

(Pause.)

Did you quarrel?

(Beat.)

LILY: I told her.

BLANCHE: Told her what?

(Beat.)

(Senses something) Told her what.

(Blanche freezes.)

Why would you do that.

(Beat.)

LILY: I wanted to prepare her.
BLANCHE: For:
LILY: When we go //
BLANCHE: *Go?*
LILY: To *Chicago.*

(Beat.)

BLANCHE *(Faint exasperation)*: I don't have that job yet darling.
LILY: You basically have the job.
BLANCHE: I don't have the job, I told you // I'm—
LILY *(Smiles confidently)*: But you'll get it, or you'll get something, it doesn't matter //
BLANCHE *(Snaps)*: It *matters.*

(Pause.)

You understand what you did? The ramifications? He's gonna haul me right out on my ass the second he finds out.

(Lily looks at her, bemused.)

LILY: But—you don't even *want* to stay here.
BLANCHE: *Want?* What I "want"? what does that have to do with anything?

LILY: But we can't stay, not after he—

BLANCHE: Do you know what it is to have nothing? You know how many times I packed my suitcase in the past six months!?

LILY: But—he hit me //

BLANCHE (*Snaps*): So *what* You think I ain't been *hit* before?!

(*Lily tentatively goes to Blanche.*)

LILY (*Deep, profound tenderness*): I won't let anything happen to you.

(*Blanche slowly turns to Lily; those eyes; it's heartbreaking. A short pause.*)

BLANCHE (*Toughness beginning to melt*): How you gonna protect me. You just a kid.

(*Short pause.*)

LILY: I *will.*

(*Blanche looks at Lily. She touches Lily's cheek. Softens. Blanche sees herself in Lily's eyes. It's mesmerizing. She smiles a faint smile, tinged with sadness.*)

BLANCHE (*Undercurrent of deep worry*): Know how stupid I was at seventeen? That's when I left home . . . took me years before I figured out what I was doing with my life.

(*Beat.*)

LILY (*Sweetly encouraging*): And now you're almost *there.*

(*Blanche snaps back into the moment. Nods affirmatively, but it's detached. Her eyes fill with worry, her voice gets a bit higher here:*)

BLANCHE *(Deep fear, almost a whisper)*: But the world's a dangerous *place*.

LILY: I'm not scared.

(Blanche is faraway.)

BLANCHE *(Gently and not just pain, sorrow)*: You *say* that but you don't know what it's like. *(Beat)* You can be hurt and *never* recover. *(Pause; then to herself)* You think you can end it but it don't end.

LILY: But—you're telling me I have to make *choices*.

BLANCHE *(Snapping out of it)*: But // not

LILY: You're saying don't be a victim— //

BLANCHE *(A shift)*: I'm. No— //

LILY: That's what *you* // said!

(Blanche turns on Lily quite suddenly; it's ferocious but she is very still, focused.)

BLANCHE *(Taut, tense)*: *No* I'm saying *stay*—stay and *fight* for something. You gotta take up the damn cudgels, not run away! *(Beat)* You can walk out that door but you never really leave! You think you do—but you come back to the *same thing* again and again! You need to meet it head on!

(Pause.)

LILY *(Imploring, confused)*: You promised me we'd leave.

(Blanche looks at Lily—another shift, 180 degrees. Her heart melting, she's instantly filled with guilt over her outburst.
Blanche—in a single gesture—grabs Lily tight, holds her for dear life.)

[STOP]

(Blanche quickly, hungrily covers her with kisses, she's filled with need. Then—abruptly, she stops, looks at Lily, holding her shoulders.)

BLANCHE *(Pain still seeping through, fearful)*: I know honey I know . . . but we gotta look at reality here.

LILY: You're the one not looking at reality!

BLANCHE: We can't just leave, sweetie.

LILY *(Desperate to convince her)*: I have money saved up. We can live on that //

BLANCHE: Yeah and then what?!

(Pause.)

LILY *(Shakily)*: But . . . I have to make the right choice now . . . That's what you told me, I have to take the right actions.

(Blanche cannot make eye contact with her.)

BLANCHE *(Impossibly vulnerable)*: I just can't . . .

LILY: Of *course* you can.

(Lily grasping at straws:)

This is—this is just *irony* . . . You don't need to be here . . . It's—it's just . . . *funny.*

(Lily forges a tiny smile, wishing away the whole nightmare.)

BLANCHE *(Almost in tears, very tiny)*: I c-can't—I can't— make myself into what I—w-what you need me to *be.*

(Pause. Lily looks at her, perplexed.)

LILY: But . . . I don't want you to *make* yourself—into // anything I

BLANCHE: LOOK AT ME! I'M A FUCKING FAILURE, WHAT DO YOU WANT FROM ME?!

LILY: That's not true . . . I look up to you //

(Lily goes to comfort her; Blanche flinches, angry.)

BLANCHE: Because you don't know anything! Of course I glitter when you look at me! You don't have anything to compare it to! *You have no life experience.* Are you *joking?* *(Pause)* You *child.* *(Beat. She grabs her face)* Look at me: I'm forty-fucking-three years old I'm cleaning *houses* on my hands // and knees

LILY: But you're working // on

BLANCHE: *No! NO I can't work anymore!* I'm at the *end* of it, do you understand? I can't *do it anymore* I'm *tired!*

LILY: But //

BLANCHE *(A quick explosion)*: I'M-TIRED!

(A deafening silence. They both stand, frozen.)

LILY *(Quiet humiliation)*: I'm . . . trying to have more . . . life experiences.

(We see a smile spread slowly across Blanche's face. Her countenance changes completely. They're saved.)

BLANCHE: It's fine. We don't gotta make a deal out of it. *(Bright)* As Bubbles Sills used to say: leave the drama on the stage.

(Lily looks at her.)

(Forced smile, girlishness) We just have to call your sister, tell her it was a joke, kay?

LILY: She won't believe that.

BLANCHE: Say it was a gag //

LILY: But—

BLANCHE: Say it was a // gag then kissy kiss make

LILY: No.

BLANCHE: up and drop the whole // thing.

LILY: *She won't believe that //*

BLANCHE *(Strained sweetness, smile)*: Just call her.

LILY: I //

BLANCHE *(Spasm of rage)*: CALL HER!

(Long pause.
Blanche stands there, closes her eyes; she's exhausted. It's as
if her entire history has finally caught up with her here. She
grasps on to a piece of furniture, to stablize herself.)

LILY *(Sweet, sad)*: I don't want to drop the whole thing.

[STOP]

BLANCHE: We can't do this.

LILY *(Tearful, crushed)*: We can

BLANCHE: No. We can't.

LILY *(Soft)*: *Why?*

(Pause.)

(Paralyzed with grief and confusion) So what was what
was this? You were telling me things. Why? because
I'm—gullible?

BLANCHE: That // ain't it.

LILY: Taking my money? // You knew I'd

BLANCHE: This is not a sustainable *relationship.*

LILY *(Hurt)*: WHY?

BLANCHE *(Passionately)*: Because I want you to be HAPPY
and you WONT with ME.

LILY: I am happy with you.

BLANCHE *(Gently)*: It's not real. It's fake.

LILY: It isn't fake!

(A tortured and very ashamed Blanche looks away from Lily as she starts to crumble.)

BLANCHE: I can't fix you, I can't f-fix myself—

(Lily is lost, in disbelief. A long unbroken silence.)

LILY: I. I just told my *sister*.

(Beat.)

BLANCHE: Call her and tell her you // were
LILY: SHE WON'T BELIEVE THAT!

[STOP]

BLANCHE: She will. She will—just—

(Lily gets her coat, etc.)

Where are you going? //
LILY: I don't know.
BLANCHE *(Increasing panic)*: Sweetie—don't—don't leave. Let's—we can figure something out.
LILY *(Weakly, barely able to speak)*: Why.
BLANCHE *(Urgent, grasping for words)*: Let me—Let me help you.
LILY: You want to "help me." "I help you . . . and you help me."

*(In an instant Lily jumps to the conclusion that she's unearthed the whole horrible truth about this relationship. Something's dying in her.
Pause. The whole thing slows down.)*

(Weakly, quiet) Could I get my money back.

(Blanche looks at her, startled. A pause.)

BLANCHE *(Fearful)*: What?

LILY: The money I gave you. I need it back.

BLANCHE *(Grasping)*: I can't—I can't get that I already used it.

LILY: For what.

BLANCHE *(Panicked)*: You know that—I used it, I paid my loans.

(Pause.)

You gave me a check.

*(Lily slowly lifts her head to meet Blanche's gaze.
Long silence.
Then, finally:)*

LILY *(Quiet, through tears)*: You are *so. Dead.*

(Blanche looks at her, terrified. A pause.)

BLANCHE *(Fear)*: What are you talking about? You gave me a *check.*

(Pause. Lily slowly turns away from Blanche. She's palpably alone.)

LILY *(Completely helpless)*: You're *tricking* me.

(Lily, in a daze, tries to gather her things.)

BLANCHE *(Frenetic)*: Wait //

LILY *(Vulnerable)*: You're *tricking* me I // know you are

BLANCHE *(Desperate, pleading)*: Lily come on—

*(Lily storms out.
Blanche just stands there, very still.
Long, long silence.
Blanche dazedly looks around the room, tries to orient herself. She sees a rag, picks it up, trying to snap out of it.*

She looks for the caddy, sees it, walks to it, picks up the windex, still unsteady.
She walks to a mirror, sprays the windex, wipes it with a rag.
As she is wiping, she catches her reflection in the mirror.
She is transfixed by her own image.
She stretches out her arm as if holding a gun.
She sprays the windex, watches the liquid drip down, waits a moment.
She sprays again, waits another moment.
Sprays again.
Again.
Again, again, faster and faster as the liquid drips down the mirror and her face becomes a blur.)

6.

A diner. Muzak is playing lightly in the background. We hear the muffled voices of other diners, clanking silverware.
Lily is sitting alone at a booth. She is miserable. She wears sunglasses and a fur coat.
Shelly enters with Claudine. She's wearing a "Chairman Mao" suit she purchased in China.
A pause.

SHELLY *(Brusque)*: What.

(Pause.)

I'm here, what.
LILY: I . . .

[STOP]

SHELLY: WHAT.
LILY: I. I just.

(Lily takes off her sunglasses. Her eyes are completely red, tears are streaming down her face. Her voice sounds oddly high; she speaks from the back of her throat, very frail.)

SHELLY: You what?
LILY: I stopped taking *(Pause)* I—
SHELLY: WHAT.

(She's crying and can't get the words out.)

LILY: I stopped taking . . . my . . .
SHELLY: You what?
LILY: My . . .
SHELLY: I can't hear what you're saying.
LILY: I // s-s-sstopped
SHELLY: OK, look I'm gonna // go
LILY: My PILL.

(Beat.)

I stopped taking . . . my . . . my pill I. I stopped—I stopped taking my *pill* I . . .

*(Lily attempts a hopeful smile, even a conspiratorial giggle. Shelly just looks at her.
Lily earnestly takes Shelly's hand.
Shelly just stands there.)*

(Trying, to no avail, to be conversational): I . . . I . . .

*(Lily releases quiet, helpless sobs. She looks down ashamed. Shelly stands, observing: neither cruel nor compassionate, but almost anthropological, as if this is a new, unfamiliar, alien specimen.
Lily weakly releases Shelly's hand. It drops back to her side.
The lights dim very slowly on Lily's sobbing.)*

Act Three

Para Los Muertos

1.

Living room. The vase of dead chrysanthemums is replaced by fresh flowers, bright green in color, and supplemented with a few other vases, also of brightly colored flowers. Blanche is listening to music.
Ike enters. She senses someone—turns, thinking it's Lily. It's him. He picks up the remote, turns off the radio.

IKE: Whatcha doin?

BLANCHE: I was listening to that.

IKE: Chillin? *(Snaps his fingers)* Chillin out? *(Snaps his fingers)*

BLANCHE: I'm taking a *break*. I'm legally entitled // to

IKE: Legally //

BLANCHE: breaks, yeah, that's right you're legally entitled to things.

IKE: Are you interested in the Law, Anna Marie?

BLANCHE: The name's Blanche.

IKE: Ya know My dad loved the Law: *true*. *(Pause)* He was a
    very great man.
BLANCHE: (Want somm to // drink?)
IKE *(Produces a picture of him)*: He's my spittin image.

(Shows her.)

That's a derby hat, from the old times, check that out:
he was a sharp dresser wasn't he? he used to work in
textiles. He built himself from the ground up and then
they wrecked him. They pillaged him, they stole the rug
out from under him He died with nothing; and he had
greatness in him. *(Beat. Saccharine smile)* But that's how
people are. Wouldn't you agree?
BLANCHE: Uh-huh.

*(She smiles a strained smile, looks away. He puts the pho-
tograph back in his wallet.)*

IKE: I get the sense you don't like me.

*(He walks to the fishbowl.
Ike feeds Kitty.)*

Kitty likes me. *(To Kitty)* Hiiiiiiiiiieeeeeeeeeee.

(Blanche anxiously watches him feed Kitty.)

BLANCHE *(Attempting to finesse it)*: Kitty likes the new algae
    I can tell.
IKE: Look at that look That's love.
BLANCHE *(Trying to impress him, nervous)*: You know actually
    goldfish *can't* love. Neuronally speaking I mean They
    aren't wired for it.
IKE *(Quiet, coiled)*: Do-you-know-what-love-is?
BLANCHE *(Plastering on a smile)*: It's—so // subjective

IKE *(Explosion)*: SO-DON'T-SPEAK-FA-FISH!

(Blanche holds the smile, rather tensely, slowly swivels back.)

[STOP]

BLANCHE: I // think
IKE: Why don't you go out on dates?

(Beat.)

BLANCHE: Pardon?
IKE: *Dates?* With *boys?*

(Beat.)

BLANCHE: I don't know that that's relevant to my job.

(He scrutinizes her. She thumbs through a magazine, noticeably unnerved.)

IKE: You won't look me in the eye; why's that?

(She turns to him.)

BLANCHE: Look you // in
IKE: You look my wife in the eye Why's that.

[STOP]

BLANCHE: I'm sorry?

(Beat.)

IKE: Are you?
BLANCHE: What?

IKE: Sorry?

[STOP]

BLANCHE *(Laughs)*: OK, this is slightly—uh //
IKE *(Shift, more intense)*: See these *rivets*? On these jeans? These are like *eyes*. My eyes are *rivets*. I have eyes all over my *person*. I can see everything . . . There isn't a THING you can hide from me.
BLANCHE *(Tense smile)*: Uh. I don't know what you mean.

(Pause.)

IKE: So you a *college* girl, huh?
BLANCHE: That's right.

(Ike looks at her, smiles.)

IKE: Nope!
BLANCHE: What?
IKE: Never went to college.

(Beat. She smiles brightly, heightening the performance.)

BLANCHE *(Glib)*: Uhh: I went to Princeton then Brown Got a PhD //
IKE *(Plainly)*: Don't waste my time, arite? I had you checked out.

(Beat.)

BLANCHE *(Laughs)*: Um. I think *you* a little checked-out, cuz this is kinda over tha top.
IKE: Why you cleanin my toilets you got a Ph fuckin D, huh?
BLANCHE *(Rolling her eyes)*: I wuz in Paris a bunch a years; I'm not acclimatized // to

IKE *(Hard sarcasm)*: Oh not // "acclimatized"

BLANCHE: I reject // establishment—

IKE *(Laughing)*: You know you act like you're so much better than me You're not even *educated*!

BLANCHE: I speak four languages //

IKE *(Unfettered exasperation)*: YEAH! *BULLSHIT!* AND THREE OTHAHS!

[STOP]

(Blanche artifices a cheshire cat smile. A shift here.)

BLANCHE: Sounds like you a little jealous.

IKE: Of what.

BLANCHE: Me.

(Ike laughs softly.)

IKE *(Sarcasm)*: Well . . . now that you mention it I actually always *dreamed* a bein a career criminal // so

BLANCHE *(Plainly)*: But you *are* a criminal.

[STOP]

IKE *(Staccato, quiet)*: (You got a big mouth You know that.)

BLANCHE *(Shakes her head no)*: Ain't my fault. Tried to make yourself inta somethin and ya failed. It happens.

(Ike chortles to himself.)

IKE *(Tries to make a joke out of it)*: I'm a failure?

BLANCHE *(A shift from caustic to a bit more plaintive)*: You thought you could be anything you wanted. Tried to make yourself a whole other person. Kicked screamed all you wanted Din matter It's the System. *(To herself)* You don't got a choice in it. Don't matter what you do Gonna crush you anyhow.

(Ike looks at her—this all resonates uncannily with him. It freaks him out—he pushes back whatever fear she draws out of him.)

IKE *(Bravado, smiling)*: I'm a failure? You're funny. I made two hundred grand in one year: NET! You think you'll ever see money like that? You're a joke. Look at this HOUSE—

BLANCHE *(Pointed, almost prescient)*: This *house*. You know what this house is? A *casket*. A big *ugly* casket That's what you built. *(Beat)* An you'll die in it.

(His smile fades. Pause.)

IKE *(Pretends to be impervious)*: What about you? How you gonna die Huh? *(Beat; then steely)* Bet I can guess.

(An impasse. She turns to leave, he stops her.)

Oh, and by the way? We *are* white; people of Spanish descent are *Caucasian*, I looked it up.

(She turns to him.)

BLANCHE *(Sarcasm)*: Congratulations.

(She starts to exit.)

IKE *(Fake pleasantry)*: Oh one more thing:

*(She stops in her tracks.
Doesn't turn to look at him.)*

BLANCHE: What's that.

IKE *(Coy)*: How do I say this: uh—do you know a guy named Richard Nesbitt?

(On the words "Richard Nesbitt" Blanche becomes very still. Her breathing becomes unsteady. She doesn't look at him. Ike takes in her reaction. She slowly shuts her eyes, the cells in her body are dying, one at a time. Her composure begins to crack.)

From Philly? Rich Nesbitt? *(Pause)* It's kinda sad actually. Couple months back his own daughter tried to shoot him, just left him there. He coulda died. Cops are lookin for her.

(He walks to her very very slowly, a spider trapping its prey.)

(Gets very close to her) Why do you think she'd do somethin like that huh?

(Pause.)

BLANCHE *(Deep sadness, almost a whisper)*: Thought I could
    end it . . . *(To herself, a recognition)* but it don't end.
IKE *(Clueless)*: End what?

(Long pause. A smile slowly spreads across his face; he's openly gloating.)

Guess you just got that criminal instinct, huh?

(Her expression changes. Her lips curl into a tiny, taut smile. She turns to him.)

BLANCHE: Criminal instinct Yeah That must be it. *(Smiles ironically)* Must be a relief fa you Huh? I make sense to you now? *(Tiny laugh)* Oh I know what you thinking. Think I don't? Guess what: I built my whole LIFE around what you think a me ALL OF YOU! *(Tiny smile again; then quick)* You-think-I-don't-see-it? Think-I-don't-bash-my-*head*-against-the-wall-seein-it-every-damn-day-a-my-*life*?

[STOP]

(The pain mounting here) That's why I made my own raw materials, *had* none Had to make somm up What else I *got*? No wallpaper on my walls *Flash cards* . . . Kant . . . Aristotle . . .

IKE *(Affectless)*: Wow great story Maybe when you get to prison you can write ya memoirs— //

(He walks determinedly to the phone, picks up the receiver. She goes after him, lunges impulsively—grabs the phone from him. She's shaking, panicked, not sure what's next.)

[STOP]

(Looking out, quiet but tense) Gimme the phone.

(Blanche just stands there, shaking, terrified, cornered. It's a complete impasse. An extremely tense silence.)

BLANCHE *(Faking bravery, but it's hard)*: She *loves* me.

(A beat. He slowly turns to her, dumbfounded—it's true and he knows it, sees it in her. Just saying the words jolts her out of the moment, slowly transports her. A realization:)

(Almost radiant) Don't matter what you do . . . cuz she loves *me*.

(Blanche smiles softly. Ike's humiliation starts to morph into a quiet, frightening rage.)

[STOP]

(Ike grabs Blanche by the hair. Hard. In a single gesture he jerks his arm to his side; she goes crashing down with it, screaming, dropping the phone. Ike drags Blanche over to the paint trough.)

(Terrified) I'm—NO!!

(In one gesture he shoves her face in it. Hard. He holds her head down—suffocating her.
She tries to scratch his face, hit him, but he pins her hand down. He finally lifts her head up.)

NO! NO—

(He shoves her head back into the paint trough, pushing her face hard into the pan.
After a long while Blanche stops struggling.
He pulls her head out, releases her body.
She's coughing, spitting out paint, no energy, shaking, wiping white paint out of her eyes, her face, her hair.
Ike slowly rises, facing a mirror. He's numb. He sees his reflection. Grows transfixed by his own image here—he's a stranger. Slowly the recognition builds, the guilt starts to surface, the awfulness.
Blanche starts to move. He turns to look at her.
He can't look at her.)

IKE *(Gruff)*: I live good.
   (Feeling welling up) I got a nice house.
   (Pushing back tears) I don't want nothin from nobody.

(Blanche looks out, reaching for transcendence with all her might.)

BLANCHE *(A sad smile)*: Candle in the window.
IKE *(Denial, anger, pushing off guilt)*: I don't hurt *nobody*.
BLANCHE *(Immersing herself in the beauty of her own vision)*:
House in Wicker Park. Books homes trees.

(Pause.)

Stars in the sky.

(The space has transformed. We're in Blanche's room. Blanche sits alone. It's dark except for a soft light.)

2.

We hear foosteps descending down a staircase into the base-ment. Blanche hears it. She looks toward the door, wipes paint off her face, sits up expectantly. She is working to push past her humiliation, but it won't leave.
Lily opens the door to Blanche's room.
A shaft of light illuminating the two of them.
Lily's hair is different—swept up.
She tries to make herself impervious to Blanche's pain here but keeps being thrown off balance by the fierce longing and sad-ness welling up in her.

BLANCHE *(Smiling expectantly)*: I wuz hoping you'd find me.

(Pause.)

LILY *(Breathing unsteadily)*: The decorator's coming tomor-row. We're turning your room into a nursery.

(Pause.)

BLANCHE: You're. *(Pause)* That's //
LILY: He'll be here at ten. Pack up.

BLANCHE *(Flicker of hope)*: *Wait—I—*
LILY: We're not calling the police.

(Pause. Blanche summons the courage to speak.)

BLANCHE *(With difficulty; comes from a wounded, raw place)*:
I *love* you.

(Silence.)

LILY *(Not looking at her)*: You left this in my room.

(She tosses a book onto the bed.)

BLANCHE *(Painful admission)*: I never *been* in love before . . .
I'm forty-three years old I never been in love wit *nobody.*

*(We see Lily look at her. Her heart is breaking. Slowly, we
watch her work to stamp back the feeling.)*

LILY: Do you have my money.

(Pause.)

BLANCHE: I'll. I'll get it for you I—here I got . . . some of it I //

*(She rushes to her wallet—holds up a wad of cash—ex-
tends her arm.
Long pause.
Lily starts to melt a bit. Blanche looks at her, hopeful.)*

LILY *(Tentative)*: What was the money for?

(Beat.)

BLANCHE: I . . . borrowed from the wrong people . . . they were
threatening // me They

LILY *(Snapping back)*: Do you know what you are?

(Pause.)

A good *teacher*. I was *lacking*; I never learned any *lessons*.

(The emotion starts to build.)

Now I have
Life
Experience.

[STOP]

BLANCHE *(Quick)*: I'll get you the rest a the money I // just
LILY *(Quiet, raw pain, looks down, fists clenched)*: I-don't-give-a-shit-about-the-money.

[STOP]

(Lily composes herself; stands erect, like a statue.)

BLANCHE *(Speaks quickly)*: I'll tell you anything you wanna know—*ask* me—anything . . .

(Beat.)

LILY: The decorator's coming tomorrow at ten, you have to clear out.

(Lily won't look at her—she could crumble, but she won't. Lily quickly makes her way to the door.)

BLANCHE *(Desperate plea)*: Look back!

(Lily freezes.)

Look: BACK.

(Beat.)

(A whisper) Mira hacia atrás, no me conviertas en piedra.

(A long pause. Lily hesitates, then leaves.)

Coward.

(Beat.)

I DON'T NEED YOU.

(Silence.)

(To herself, deeply unconvinced; she's sinking) I'll come out on top. I always knew I was meant for greatness. Deep inside A little voice I knew . . . I knew . . .

(She looks around at the cage she's built.)

(Quiet) Help me.

(She smiles a sad smile.)

(Plainly) I made bad choices . . . *(Fighting tears) I made bad choices.*

3.

A split scene:
On one part of the stage:
Ike and Lily.
That same evening.
Their bedroom.

He is finishing his pushups; Lily is at her vanity, combing her hair.

On another:

Blanche/Iris is alone in her basement room, packing her things, but very laxly. As she packs she composes a letter in her mind to "bell."

Bits of white paint still caked on her face.

She puts on a CD, a piece of Sibelius's, which plays softly in the background; a beautiful, lush, sad piece of music.

The realities overlap and merge here—there are no more discrete spaces, levels, it's all collapsed.

Lily brushes her hair, counting the strokes, beginning at forty-two, under her breath.

Ike is doing pushups, counting, beginning at seventy.

LILY: Sixty-four, sixty-five, sixty-six //

IKE: Ninety-two, ninety-three //

LILY: sixty-seven //

IKE: sixty-eight, sixty-nine //

BLANCHE: The food at Gagnaire was perfect that night wasn't it, bell? // He does wonders with radishes wouldn't you say? *Wonders*

IKE: *seventy.*

(He slumps to the floor exhausted. The music plays.)

LILY: seventy-one, seventy-two, seventy-three //

IKE *(Frustrated; down to Blanche)*: Fuckin *music* Turn that shit off!

LILY: seventy-four, seventy-five //

BLANCHE: I prefer him to Robuchon (although the potatoes at Robuchon oh my // *god*)

IKE *(Gingerly, very careful)*: Whadja do today?

LILY: seventy-six, seventy-seven, seventy-eight, seventy-nine, eighty, eighty-one //

IKE: Honey?

LILY: eighty-tw— *(Beat. Abstracted)* What.

(The music continues to play. Ike looks at Lily.)

IKE: Did you have a good day?
LILY: I went // to the
BLANCHE *(Rapt)*: Oh // and *remember*
IKE *(Screams to basement/Blanche; fillip of rage)*: SHUT-
THE-*FUCK*-UP.

(Nearly, but not quite simultaneously:
Blanche jerks her head to the left, gasps, frightened—it's
the ghost. The physical vocabulary here is identical to
Lily's earlier in the play. She looks about the room, jarred.
Lily jumps, drops her brush. Her face remains oddly ex-
pressionless.)

(Super sweet smile) Oh, honey, did I scare you? I—I'm
so sorry I didn't mean to do that . . . I don't ever want to
scare you.

(He picks up her brush, hands it to her.)

Whaddayou say sweetheart?

(Beat.)

LILY: What? *(Pause)* It's not important.

(Blanche calms herself down, returns to the fantasy.)

IKE *(Working to be attentive)*: No no no—it's important. I wan-
na know, I'm interested in what you do.
LILY *(Not responsive)*: I had lunch.
BLANCHE: And the wines // (aha-ha)
IKE: Who'd you go with?

LILY: No one. I went by myself.

(She's staring in the mirror holding her brush.)

IKE: You OK?
LILY: I like being by myself.

(Blanche smiles—laughs quietly to herself for a moment.)

IKE: You look nice //

(He smiles. Lily doesn't.)

BLANCHE: But that waiter He told me it was a Crozes Her-
  mitage C-R-O and AHA-HA and I must have looked //
  confused because
IKE: What'd you do somethin to ya hair I like it.
BLANCHE: because he . . .

*(Blanche mumbles the rest to herself, giggles to herself qui-
etly, packs.
Lily looks at Ike.)*

LILY: I don't want a live-in.
IKE: What.

(Beat.)

LILY: A girl. *(Beat)* I can clean my own house.
IKE: We could get a day workah.
LILY: People steal.

(Beat.)

IKE: Whatever you want, it's . . . it's your decision, honey.
LILY *(Abstracted)*: Thank you.

(Pause.)

IKE: You're letting em get to you.

LILY: No.

BLANCHE *(Bright)*: I think Luce has a mind like a magnet.
And we're like little iron filings she draws to her //

IKE *(Jarred)*: People got short memories //

BLANCHE: We're // helpless

IKE: It'll all be in the past.

(Lily turns to him. She looks at him.)

LILY: No. It *won't*.

BLANCHE: We're helpless but // that's

IKE *(Screaming, upset, no control)*: YEAH-IT-WILL.

(Blanche gasps, jerks her head left; looks around the room, terrified.
Recovering himself, Ike gets behind Lily, talking to her reflected image in the mirror.)

Anyways-screw-them-we-don-need-them-you-think-we-need-them? We don't need nothin from nobody.

(Beat.)

We got each other . . . Love is powerful . . . *Power //*

BLANCHE *(A terrified whisper)*: *What-are-you?*

(Lily jerks her head quickly to the side—she's seen something. Blanche jumps.)

[STOP]

LILY: I just saw it again.

(Beat.)

IKE: Saw // what.
BLANCHE: *Who's there?*

(Beat. In the short silence Blanche, in a single gesture, pulls the gun from the suitcase. She holds her arms at her side. Stands very still, alert.)

LILY: A face I saw it . . . it was . . .

*(Ike starts laughing.
She turns to him, looks at him—his cruelty is astonishing.)*

IKE: Ya didn't see anything.

(Lily looks at him, not quite understanding.)

LILY *(Somewhat dazedly)*: I saw a face . . .

(Ike walks over to her; her discombobulation makes him laugh harder.)

IKE *(Through laughter)*: Honey: I was playin a trick on you.

*(Lily just looks at him. She's sinking. Ike tries to stifle the laughter.
Blanche shudders.)*

BLANCHE: WHO'S-THERE?

(Points the gun.)

IKE: There's no ghost.
LILY *(Dying inside)*: *What?* //
BLANCHE *(Terrified)*: *Get-outta-here! You-don't-exist!*

*(Ike laughs—a private joke with himself.
Blanche pivots, points the gun.)*

IKE *(Laughter building)*: I was having fun witchu!

(Lily looks at Ike—practically looking through him. Her loneliness is palpable, she's faraway.)

Wha? *Don't look at me like that.*

(Blanche shudders, gasps audibly, as if someone's grabbed her from behind.)

C'mere— //
BLANCHE *(Deep frustration, exhaustion)*: *I ain't scared a you!* YOU-DON'T-EXIST!

(Ike kisses Lily's neck from behind. Music fades.)

(Ferocious, desperate) I-AIN'T-SCARED-A-YOU!

(Ike slowly removes Lily's clothes—she is very still. Her eyes are frozen.
Blanche's bravado falters.
She releases the gun weakly, it falls to the ground. She covers her eyes with her hand, weeps helplessly. The lights begin to fade.)

(To herself, weeping) It don't end . . .

(We hear a car horn faintly in the distance.)

It don't end—I can't end it I can't . . . I can't
I can't . . .

(On the last "can't" we hear the car horn again, louder this time, two short beeps.)

I can't . . .

I can't . . .
I can't . . .

(We hear the car horn again, much louder, one long beep—
it cuts off her last "can't," as the lights go to black.
Once we hit total darkness there's a beat. Then:
Two loud beeps.
A pause.
One loud long beep.
On the last beep, lights come up on Lily halfway down the
stairs.
It's the next morning. Bright.
As Lily approaches the door to the basement we see
Blanche lying on the floor in a corner, face down, gun not
too far from her hand. Blood pooling around her head. She
looks incidental to the surroundings, insignificant.
Lily lingers in the stairwell, outside the door, she stands
tentatively.)

LILY *(Through the door, tentative)*: I heard something break,
did you break something?

(Pause.)

Your car's outside

(Pause.)

(Strained hauteur) You better leave your address. So we
can find you if we need you to—to pay for something.
Th-th-there's expensive things in there.

(In the silence she starts to fall apart—she loses her com-
portment. All her emotion comes to the surface for this one
instant, and it's pulverizing.)

(Almost a whisper) Don't f-f-forget. Don't forget // to

(The car horn honks.
Lily freezes back into her old rectilinear posture. Her face
is a mask.)

(No effect, faraway) Your car's outside.

(She slowly walks to the foot of the staircase.
Then she looks up, ascends
Lights fade to black as she reaches the top stair. Darkness.
We hear the car horn.)

END

Translation from Spanish

SPANISH: ella me decia: "Lily tú eres un angel, y tu pelo es de ceda // te quiero como mi hija"

ENGLISH: she told me: "Lily you are an angel, and your hair is silk I love you like a daughter"

SPANISH: ¡¡Yo-tambien-te-puedo-mecer-en-el-columpio-vamos-al-parque-AHORA-MISMO!!

ENGLISH: I could push you on the swing too let's go to the park right now!!

SPANISH: Todavía estamos trabajando Anna Maria la luz está a tu derecha.

ENGLISH: We're still working Anna Maria the light is on your right.

SPANISH: Yo me preocupo de esto cálmate

ENGLISH: I'll take care of this calm down

SPANISH: De nada.

ENGLISH: You're welcome.

SPANISH: Ojalá no se enoje.

ENGLISH: I hope he doesn't get mad.

SPANISH: El no se enterará.
ENGLISH: He won't find out.

SPANISH: ¿Me lastimó, // viste lo que hizo?
ENGLISH: He hurt me did you see what he did?

SPANISH: ¿Estás // bien?
ENGLISH: Are you alright?

SPANISH: Tengo que irme de aquí; promete que nos iremos.
ENGLISH: I have to get out of here; promise we'll leave.

SPANISH: Para Los Muertos
ENGLISH: For the Dead

SPANISH: Mira hacia atrás, no me conviertas en piedra.
ENGLISH: Look back, don't turn me to stone.

The Evildoers

Special Thanks

The writing of this play was made possible with funding from the Helen Merrill Foundation, the Jerome Foundation, the Ovid Foundation, and the incredibly generous patronage of Jim McCarthy, Gloria Peterson and family. The play benefited from work at the Sundance Institute Theatre Program. Thanks to Philip Himberg, Mark Subias, Morgan Jenness, Kathy Sova, Stephen Willems, everyone at MCC Theater and the Playwrights Coalition, the Playwrights' Center, Polly Carl, Paul Rusconi, Adam Greenfield, Kip Fagan, Kristen Kosmas, David Brooks, Heidi Schreck, Victoria Stewart, and the preternaturally incisive Bronwen Bitetti. Special thanks to Mame Hunt, Deb Stover and the brilliant quartet of actors with whom I was blessed to work at Sundance: Johanna Day, Carla Harting, Geoffrey Nauffts and Michael Stuhlbarg. The play, particularly the third part, benefited immensely from a workshop at the Royal Court Theatre that would never have happened were it not for the efforts of Dominic Cooke; thanks to him as well as to Lyndsey Turner, Lia Williams, Nancy Crane, Peter Sullivan and Aden Gillett. And to Raúl Esparza, Jessica Hecht, Laila Robins and Peter Frechette for their immeasurable contributions to this play in a later workshop. To James Bundy—who walks the walk and whose money is where his mouth is—and to the lovely, devoted, and deeply authentic Jennifer Kiger.

And finally an enormous thank you and sigh of relief to the magnificent Rebecca Taichman for her Jesuitical attention to, and belief in, my work.

Production History

The Evildoers was developed in part by the Sundance Institute Theatre Program in June 2006. It was directed by Rebecca Bayla Taichman; Mame Hunt was the dramaturg. The cast included:

JERRY	Geoffrey Nauffts
CAROL	Johanna Day
MARTIN	Michael Stuhlbarg
JUDY	Carla Harting

The Evildoers premiered at Yale Repertory Theatre (James Bundy, Artistic Director; Victoria Nolan, Managing Director) on January 18, 2008. It was directed by Rebecca Bayla Taichman; set design was by Riccardo Hernandez, costume design was by Susan Hilferty, lighting design was by Stephen Strawbridge, sound design was by Bray Poor; the dramaturg was Michael Walkup and the stage manager was Joanne E. McInernery. The cast included:

JERRY	Stephen Barker Turner
CAROL	Johanna Day
MARTIN	Matt McGrath
JUDY	Samantha Soule

Characters

THE THERNSTROMS

JERRY THERNSTROM: Possesses the old-world affectations and speech of an older WASP-y type, as well as the glow of narcissism and self-containment that is specific to New York psychoanalysts. Habituated to luxury and privilege—to the extent that he just blends in with it. Outwardly polite, slightly eccentric, nerdishly academic and also a little abstracted, out of touch. Has a true goofy, silly side to him and also a quietly pained detachment that—by the end of the play—opens into chaos and self-loathing. Late thirties to early forties; right before the cusp of middle age.

CAROL THERNSTROM: Jerry's wife. A wedding planner who is intensely cynical about marriage. She is quick-witted, fashionable, controlling, meticulous (i.e., *compulsive*), self-conscious, literate, and wears all this like a kind of breastplate, or armor. But deep down she knows something in her is dying, or has died; her conscience is bothering her. The discomfiture comes out as hostility. There's something childlike and untouched in her that no one sees. A woman in her forties who takes care of herself, or a woman in her mid-thirties who is aging prematurely—either way, the lines are showing.

The Goldstroms

MARTIN GOLDSTROM: Jerry's best friend from boarding school. An anesthesiologist. Has a warmth, a naifish sweetness and desire to learn. *Intensely* emotional, but tries to conceal this with varying degrees of success. Develops a deep, agonizing, insatiable spiritual longing throughout the course of the play, as well as a profound—and finally *pathological*—need to connect to people, to himself, to something authentic and rooted. Jerry's age, maybe a year younger.

JUDY GOLDSTROM: The fragile, under-confident and somewhat neurotic wife of Martin. She *works* to conceal her obsessiveness and neuroses—she's embarrassed by them; will admit to her "inappropriate" frailties out of both politeness and the need to exhibit "self-awareness." Her respect for decorum is a default. Younger than Martin.

Time

Autumn, an unspecified present.

Place

New York: A haute restaurant, the Thernstroms' Manhattan penthouse, the Goldstroms' colonial home in Westchester.

Note on Style

The tone and style of this play both undergo rather tortuous shifts. This is deliberate and in perfect keeping with the play's content. Certain ideas about Christianity and Christian Fundamentalism I borrowed (all right, stole outright) from the extraordinary Slavoj Žižek—particularly his work in *On Belief* and *The Puppet and the Dwarf.*

Also indispensable to the writing of this play was Stanley Cavell's remarkable book on the Hollywood comedy of remarriage entitled *Pursuits of Happiness.*

I am completely indebted to my conversations with my dear friend Geoffrey McDonald—whose devotion to theology and philosophy has been a touchstone and inspiration to me for the past decade. He is everywhere in this play.

The Evildoers uses several works as intertexts: *Strangers on a Train* (both Highsmith and Hitchcock), Ibsen's *The Wild Duck*, Mary Shelley's *Frankenstein*, Carl Dreyer's beautiful and mysterious *Ordet*, and Preston Sturges's *The Lady Eve*, paramount among them.

The Evildoers is in three parts:

ONE: Strangers on a Train
TWO: The Fright of Real Tears
THREE: Breaking Up

The play should be performed with an intermission after Act Two, Scene 2, and an additional short break between Acts Two and Three.

Note on Text

A double slash (//) indicates either an overlap or a jump—i.e., no break between the end of one character's speech and the beginning of the following speech (thanks Caryl Churchill).

Speech in parentheses indicates either a sidetracked thought—or footnote—within a conversation, or a shift in emphasis with *no* transition.

A [STOP] is a *(Pause)* followed by either a marked shift in tone or tempo (like a cinematic jump-cut or a quantum leap) or *no* change in tempo whatsoever—somewhat like putting a movie on *(Pause)* and then pressing play. These moments in the play are less psychological than energetic. They have a kind of focused yet unpredictable stillness, something akin to martial arts, where there is preparedness in the silence. Where a lunge or a swift kick can be delivered from seemingly out of nowhere: quickly, invisibly. Where the energy can shift dramatically in a nanosecond.

Never say marriage has more joy than pain.

—Euripides, *Alcestis*

We must all hear the universal call to like your neighbor just like you like to be liked yourself.

—George W. Bush

Act One

1.

The tail end of Jerry and Carol's anniversary dinner.
Jerry is at the same low-level drunkenness that he'll remain at through most of the play.
Judy is wearing Carol's ring, her arm extended upward.
Martin is noticeably withdrawn at the opening of the play. The scene begins at a breakneck, rapid-fire speed, lots of overlaps, etc.

JUDY: Look you can see your // reflection

JERRY: And you *know* Judy the *stones* actually are // from BURMA

CAROL: Judy: //

JERRY: And they have these *caves* //

JUDY: Wait: //

CAROL: No hold it up to the light //

JUDY *(Extending her arm a bit higher)*: Wait I think I went to Burma Is // Burma

JERRY: Oh you did //

JUDY: My father, he traveled a lot on business is Burma——? we went to all // these places

JERRY: Well they //

JUDY: Cambodia Laos //

JERRY *(Pouring drinks for himself and Carol)*: they have these MARvelous caves you see Judy they're just these *treasure* chests these *troves*, you see // they're, they're

CAROL *(Refusing Jerry's pour)*: (no thank you) //

JERRY *(Continued)*: like PIrate ships, FILLed with jewels, *brimming,*

CAROL *(To Judy)*: but it's nice isn't it //

JUDY: My arm hurts //

CAROL: If you hold it up to the light you——are you alright—— // you can

JUDY: (I'm fine.)

CAROL: see how the stones are faceted (the cut // I mean:)

JUDY *(Lowering her arm)*: I mean my arm hurts but it's OK—did you—?

CAROL: Look at the *in*set—

JUDY: what did you get Jerry?

JERRY: She got me one of those high-definition *televisions* //

JUDY: Oh //

JERRY: which is just a miracle, I mean the *colors*, the *hues*— those greens, *green* plants—I mean my *god* I've never seen such *green* plants—it's like a tropical rain forest right in my *living* room—I mean when I see a plant on television Judy I feel it photosynthesizing right on my *coffee* table!

JUDY: What brand // is it?

JERRY: And she got me some *terrific*—DVDs

JUDY: Really?

JERRY: *DVDs*, Carl Dreyer, uhhh yes, with a lot of *extras,*

JUDY: "Extras?"

JERRY: Antonioni (actually I'm delivering a paper in Geneva you know // on

JUDY: *When, oh you are?*

JERRY: It's just a little something, a little something I . . .

CAROL: He's // always

JERRY: Well it's nothing really it's—just some fluff I scribbled down on a paper napkin . . . I can't—ha ha—I can't even read my ha-ha my-my own writing.

JUDY *(Smiling politely)*: That sounds fun.

CAROL: Why.

JUDY: It just sounds fun.

CAROL: Really, that sounds fun? a bunch of middle-aged *analysts* jerking off over Monica *Vitti?*

JERRY: (Well, it's a bit more than *that* // sweetheart.)

JUDY: Monica Vitti isn't she the one—you know? I'm sorry— can I talk about this?

(Beat.)

MARTIN: About what?

JUDY: It's OK? I don't know if I'm going off topic.

MARTIN: It's OK honey just speak.

JUDY: OK, so, is Monica Vitti—she's that one with the nuclear waste?

(Martin just looks at her.)

MARTIN: The what?

JUDY: That nuclear waste? With the movie, with the nuclear waste?

JERRY: *Red Desert* //

JUDY: And she sticks her hand out—she does

(Judy imitates Monica Vitti's gesture.)

those—those—*expressive* things with the tendons

(She accidentally spills a glass—Martin gets some of it on his lap.)

in her (oh I'm *sorry*—oh let me.)

(She wipes up a bit of spilled soda with a napkin.)

I'm sorry I—are you OK honey? I'm so maladroit! A—haha—I'm so "maladroit"—isn't that funny? Isn't that a funny thing to say. "I'm maladroit"?

(Martin says nothing.)

JERRY: Now nobody's *maladroit* Judy, it's just coke Judy, it's perfectly OK.

JUDY: But—you know—three cans of coke can shut down your immune system for a whole day, did you know that?

(She laughs. No one else does.)

MARTIN: And so the idea was, what, you took your engagement ring—

CAROL: Yes

MARTIN: I didn't finish my sentence. *(Beat)* So you took it and you decided to //

JERRY *(Drunk)*: We took // it!

JUDY *(Regarding the ring)*: I love the color; the red? it's like the kind of red your eyes get when you *cry*; do you know what I mean?

CAROL: I don't cry.

JUDY *(Taking it as a joke)*: everyone cries Carol.

CAROL *(Polite smile)*: *No*, I'm more what the French call um.

[STOP]

Oh-look-it's *late* Look how late it is Jerry Oh // we need the check.

JERRY *(Sings to himself drunkenly)*: "You made me love you . . . I didn't want to do it"
(Dah dah // dah dah dah . . .)

MARTIN: Can I speak?

JUDY: Of course you can honey. *(To everyone)* He wants to speak.

(Beat.)

MARTIN: All right: so explain this to me: so you have this idea: you say "alright: let's take this engagement ring" and you // say

CAROL: Like a protective band—

MARTIN: What?

CAROL *(Retracting)*: No nothing, go on.

MARTIN: You say alright: "so" //

JERRY: "Darling:"

MARTIN: "So Jerry—OK—let's add these rubies around the diamond?" //

CAROL: But not rubies they're garnets //

MARTIN: All right // garnets

(Jerry attempts to refresh Carol's drink.)

CAROL: (No thank you darling) —not that it's really of any significance or anything but basically Jerry and I decided, you know we've been married for however many years, seven,

MARTIN: eight

CAROL: eight, that's right eight years and we just thought //

JERRY *(Munching on a petit four)*: Eight! //

CAROL: (And you know I think *dia*chronically not—) well whatever, and we thought, we said uh it'll be nice won't it to add some stones around that thing, that diamond, won't that be nice, because it's just sitting there, and it wants protection //

JERRY: "protection"

CAROL: it's lonely, it wants other stones //

JERRY *(Ebullient)*: It's a LONELY STONE!!

CAROL: And we wanted to jazz it up (OK well I hate that phrase but you know what I // mean—)

MARTIN: "Jazz it up"?

CAROL: Not—NO not in a *vulgar* way, but in a (well why, you think it's vulgar?)

MARTIN: It's your ring // Carol.

JUDY: (It's lovely)

CAROL: You think it's vulgar.

(Martin looks at her.)

What?

MARTIN: Well Carol I mean you wouldn't, say, add *arms* to the Venus de Milo would you?

CAROL: No but how do I have access to the Venus defucking Milo? // and what does

MARTIN: Well //

CAROL: it have to do with—why are you being so cryptic // and weird

MARTIN: Well I'm just thinking off the top of // my head—

CAROL: This is such a dumb // conversation

MARTIN: Because that would be—it's not dumb //

CAROL: Yes it is!

JUDY: He's stressed out.

MARTIN: I mean, yes, she's armless, but she's somehow—she's more *lovely* without arms //

JERRY: Who.

MARTIN: Because she's a symbol, she's mutilated but she's sym-BOLically "whole" and if you added arms to the Venus de Milo it would—it would be like—somehow—cutting off a normal person's arms and mutilating THEM do you see what I mean?

CAROL *(Coyly)*: Don't put pants on the piano legs Martin.

MARTIN: I'm not being clear—I know // that—

CAROL: Why don't you just say "I hate your gauche fucking ring" do you think that's going to *shatter* me—

MARTIN: That's not what I'm saying,

CAROL: *What* are you saying?

MARTIN: I'm saying—forget it it's not important—

CAROL: What.

MARTIN: You don't want to hear what I'm saying never mind.

CAROL: No I hear what you're saying you're saying I—I'm "mutilating" my ring because I added *stones* to it? That's just dumb, I don't get it //

MARTIN: Well I guess I'm just dumb.

JERRY: He's not *dumb* // darling.

MARTIN: Well for most people marriage is sacred //

CAROL: "Most people"?

MARTIN: Marriage // —*yes* most people

CAROL: For "most people" a marriage license Martin do you realize has all the stature of a *parking* ticket?

MARTIN: But don't you think that the // *linking* of *two LIVES*

CAROL *(Smiling)*: No but do you *realize* that? That it means *nothing*, that nobody gives a *shit*?

(Beat.)

JUDY: But—you're a wedding planner Carol.

CAROL: So?

MARTIN: So don't // you

CAROL: NO—do YOU find some deep existential meaning in anesthetizing people all day,

MARTIN: It's not // the same

CAROL: And what does a marriage contract *do* Martin, historically, huh, what did it do: do you know?

MARTIN: No Carol WHAT did it do?!

CAROL: It gave two members of the opposite sex *permission* to use each others sexual *organs* for pleasure. And then the woman agrees to give the children the man's name to establish paternity so he can have heirs and she does this in exchange for protection.

MARTIN: You're just crass.

CAROL: But I'm speaking from an historical vantage—

MARTIN: So //

CAROL: but now who even *wants* kids anymore, they're they're just accoutrements or. They're like little tote bags or something, they're like little cosmetic—*nuisances* or. Well-not-nuisances-(I-don't-know.)

JUDY: But you're trying to get pregnant //

CAROL: I'm just speaking editorially.

(Beat.)

MARTIN: You're so cynical.

CAROL: Well it's a cynical age and I'm the zeitgeist Let's get the check.

JUDY: (Well I want // kids.)

MARTIN: I just think you're full of shit. I do. I think you're full of shit.

(Pause.)

CAROL *(Terse smile)*: *Well*, "charmed."

(She takes a sip of her drink. It's tense.)

JUDY: He doesn't really think that—Martin—

CAROL: Well we should really be going anyway, but thank you for dinner even though I'm full of shit and everything.

MARTIN: I'm sorry—I don't know why I'm so //

CAROL: It's OK—forget it,

MARTIN: I'm // sorry

CAROL: Stop apologizing it's redundant—

JUDY *(Damage control)*: He's just stressed out.

JERRY: You know what we need old man, a good game of SQUASH.

MARTIN: What?

JERRY: Say, what are you doing *Mon*day.

MARTIN: Playing squash with you Jer.

JERRY: Splendid old man I'll reserve a court.

CAROL: Why are you stressed out?

MARTIN: I'm not stressed *out.*

CAROL: From the move?

JUDY: We're both. We're kind of exhausted ha ha ha—

JERRY *(Has been munching on petit fours all the while)*: Oh this is GOOD, oh you have to TRY // these

CAROL *(Ignoring him; to Martin)*: Is the commute bad?

MARTIN *(A discovery)*: No //

CAROL: What do you take the Cross County? //

MARTIN: The Merritt //

CAROL: OH I heard the traffic's in*suf*ferable //

MARTIN: There's //

CAROL: I told you not to leave the city, I mean I don't want to fingerwag but (well yes I do) HA HA HA (but it's—)

(As she wags her finger, Jerry tries to feed Carol a petit four. She keeps pushing him off.)

JUDY: There's boxes everywhere.

CAROL: Why?—oh with *things* in them? Oh so you're still—

JUDY: We haven't finished unpacking.

CAROL: No THANK you Jerry.

(Jerry eats the petit four.)

JERRY *(To Martin and Judy, mouthful of food)*: But you like it?

MARTIN: No.

JUDY: Yes we *do*—you're so *bad* honey. *(To Jerry and Carol)* It's very quiet, it takes time to get used to the quiet.

CAROL: I can't get to sleep without the sound of jackhammers, the construction.

(Jerry is trying to feed Carol petit fours and she keeps pushing him away over the following:)

(To Jerry) No *thank* you I don't like *almonds.*

JERRY *(Drunkenly)*: Whatever you say darling.
CAROL *(As he kisses her hand)*: Don't do that.
JERRY *(Waggish)*: I'm in your *thrall* darling I'm *helpless.*

(He eats. Brief pause.)

MARTIN *(Essaying courage)*: You know—and I don't want to belabor the point but in China Carol //
CAROL: Mm //
MARTIN: If you get engaged to someone, in China //
CAROL: Yeah //
MARTIN: And they die before the wedding: you can still marry them.
CAROL *(Sotto voce)*: Good for China.

(Beat.)

MARTIN: But don't you think that's interesting //
CAROL: (No) //
MARTIN: You can ask for their hand in death because the Chinese people believe that marriage is eternal, that it goes on forever //
CAROL: Well the Chinese believe in a lot of things going on forever, don't they, like certain forms of *torture.*
JERRY: But we'd like to be Chinese darling.
CAROL: Well I wouldn't like to be Chinese, I'm happy being American.
JERRY: Even though they're *eclipsing* us?
CAROL: Who //
JERRY: The CHINESE!!
CAROL: Oh bullshit.
JERRY: They are Carol, they're the new *empire.*
CAROL *(Speaks quickly)*: I love all this catastrophizing people do: "new empire"—people //
JERRY: Well //

CAROL: (It's such bullshit) people are so. I mean YES we're sinking—but the sinking can go on for eons and nothing changes, America was *always* middlebrow, it's *always* been vulgar, and people are so //

JUDY: But //

CAROL: And WE hold it up—"we" being the intelligentsia, the cultured elite, progressive thinkers!

JUDY *(Tickled)*: Oh *Carol*, you're so elitist.

CAROL: Oh Judy, you're so annoying; HA HA HA HA. I'm just kidding. *(Beat; she takes a sip of wine; then speaking briskly)* No but you know what we're like, we're like *barges:* and we're holding up these big pyramids of *garbage*—and for a couple hundred years it was OK—until one day the garbage started to *multiply.* And it got more fetid, and more awful. And the barges began to *sink* under the weight; and now we're all just SINKING. *(Smiles, triumphal)* But sinking can go on for a long time, we can go on like this in*def*initely.

MARTIN: I don't know about *that.* //

CAROL *(Dismissive)*: (Oh you don't know about *any*thing.) //

MARTIN: But isn't this the naive American fantasy—"Oh it'll all be OK" when you know it won't // be

CAROL *(Looking at him)*: OK this is what I'm hearing *bluh bluh bluh*—

JUDY *(Plastering a smile)*: That's a very negative way to look at things Martin.

MARTIN: Well that's how it is Judy empires rise and fall.

JUDY: I just think you're being *negative.* When you say things you're wishing for them, they're wishes? Or. Like in *Peter Pan?* you know like when that bird dies and all the children say "I believe, I believe." //

CAROL: What // bird

JUDY: Or no they clap //

CAROL: Tinkerbell?

JUDY: "I believe."

CAROL: It's not a bird, it's a // *fairy.*

JUDY: And also, I think it's a political thing.

(They all just look at her. Judy turns five shades of purple.)

CAROL: What.
JUDY *(Slightly unnerved)*: What we were saying before about. You know—it's a political thing.

(They all wait for an explanation. The silence is unbearable.)

It's like—the climate? You know what I mean?
CAROL: *No.*
JUDY: Well—I can't explain it.
CAROL: Well if you can't explain it then what are you talking about?
JUDY: I just—I know what I'm trying to say but I. I can't put it into words?
CAROL *(Fake, frozen smile)*: Well Judy: do you know what thoughts are? Thoughts are little *words* you know that Judy and you *string* the words together and THAT'S how you get THOUGHTS; I mean if you don't have *words* you don't *have* thoughts.
JUDY: I have thoughts.
JERRY: She has thoughts Carol everyone // has
CAROL: I'm not *saying* she doesn't think, I'm saying she has no thoughts on this particular *issue* // as evidenced by
JERRY *(To Carol)*: Sometimes thoughts are a bit more nascent darling, a bit more—*unformed*; thoughts are delicate, they need time to gestate, like how the grit of sand inside the oyster becomes the pearl darling—you see? That—*nacreous* shell—right Judy?

(Judy just smiles, strained.)

CAROL *(Mean)*: Will you stop smiling! *(Breaks out in unexpected, teasing laughter)* I'M JUST KIDDING!

JUDY: Oh.

(They laugh.)

You scared me!

(Beat.)

CAROL: *I* feel like a shell! Ha ha ha.
JUDY: Oh—ha ha // You're so bad. You're so FUNNY. You're
　　so BAD // Carol
JERRY: "We bad" //
CAROL: *I* feel like a shell. *(Beat)* HA HA HA I'm kidding.
JERRY: "We bad" what's that from
JUDY: ("We bad")

(She takes a sip of wine.)

I'm so full. I'm very full from the meal.
MARTIN: You hardly touched your fish.
JUDY: Well I'm on weight watchers
CAROL: *Weight* watchers?
JUDY: I used up my points, hake is eight points and I had half.
CAROL: You don't need to lose weight.
MARTIN: I tell her that.
JUDY *(Sort of hysterical)*: Well—I mean I feel simply *uphol-*
　　stered in my dress, my clothes are so tight, it's all it's all
　　stretched and—ruined My whole—wardrobe is . . .

[STOP]

JERRY *(Eating)*: Well you know the *nice* thing about thin
　　people Judy is they don't take up much room. And then
　　there's so much *more* room for other *people. (He licks his*
　　fingers) I find them— *(Mouthful of food)* very

(Carol waits for him to finish.)

CAROL *(To everyone; a good-bye)*: Well it was // fun

JERRY *(Emphatic, drunken slurring)*: and I mean—isn't this the WHOLE PROBLEM? I mean . . . people don't want to *know* each other: I mean—everyone *lurches* around, knocking into each other like little toy *cars*. And that's the problem with the whole world, And they're *lurching* all over the place! Th-Th-Th— Because people aren't *authentic*, that's the problem you know There's no *authenticity*. You know what I mean Martin, I mean *right?* And-nn-Er. you know they're all circling this—terrible abyss of uh uh pain. And—it's *our* job to get in*side* of that you see? because—I mean if we can't *enter* people's suffering then *we* suffer. Because we're disconnected from their lives: and *their* lives *are* our lives—but we don't want to *see* that. And then we in*flict* suffering!

JUDY: But—*whose* lives are our lives?

JERRY *(Gets lost for a moment)*: Well just *every*one, what do you mean *WHO* //

CAROL: "Everyone" //

JERRY: The *Other* //

JUDY: Like, people in other countries? // or

JERRY: in *other* countries, in *this* country—in this *rest*aurant, they're suffering but no one wants to *enter* it But what can we do? what can I do What can *any* of us do I don't *know* I just keep *con*jugating the // problem!

CAROL: "enter their suffering" that's such *bullshit* you won't even let me use your *shampoo* //

JERRY: *because* darling // my *scalp*

CAROL: you won't even share your *toilet* articles with // *me*

JERRY: I have my—*flaking*—thing (anyway // it isn't the point)

CAROL *(More vehement, focused)*: and anyway these aren't benign—what do you THINK Jerry, you think the world is peopled with shepherds and milkmaids and they all //

JUDY: But //

CAROL: because in fact some people are evil

JERRY: "evil"

CAROL: I know that's unfashionable but YEAH: *evil*, yes, they torture, they—look at these Christian Funda*men*talists //

JERRY: Well *actually* darling, if I may—because I actually think it would be sort of refreshing to get to experience some *real* fundamentalism here. Because—I'm glad you mention it Carol—because I'm feeling something of a *void* in this area Carol. Because my problem, er, if you want to know the truth . . . actually I'm glad you brought this up darling—because. *(His mind goes blank for an instant)* I mean these *Christian* people: *(Leaning in, wide-eyed)* they *say* they're fundamentalists but—where *is* the fundamentalism exactly? I mean I'm *looking*: I can't seem to *find* any. Is it under the *bed*? Where is it? Is it in the *cupboard*? Because they just sort of *make* things up—"oh we're fundamentalists"—but they don't actually know the first thing about Christ, or Christian love, not the first *thing*! I mean—where are the *fundaments*?! Right Judy?

JUDY: Well—I'm Jewish // —but I

JERRY: I mean maybe what we should do is go to the fundamentalists and say "well all right: *you* think *you're* a fundamentalist? *I'll* show you who's the *real* fundamentalist!" *(Turns to Judy)* do you see what I mean Julie?

JUDY: And then what?

(Jerry freezes.)

JERRY: Well . . . I mean—we just—*stone* all the adulterers— you see and. Then we *execute* the uh. People who mix— *fabrics*—er—together—and // then

CAROL *(To Jerry)*: You don't even go to *church* //

JERRY: because the *pews* darling—my *legs*— //

CAROL: I'm tired //

JERRY: Anyways you're missing the—whole *point* darling: the fundamentalists are *suffering*

JUDY *(After a beat)*: And . . . how's that?

JERRY *(Sways drunkenly for a bit as a proxy for contemplation)*: Well . . . er—I mean they don't *know* it necessarily—but that's why they inflict it on other *people*—because that's what people do—It's all *unconscious*. *(Drinks, shrugs)* It's like analysis. Actually you know It's *just* like analysis I mean these *patients* Julie—do you think I tell them what to *do*? Hmm? I don't tell them *anything*. I don't give any *advice*—I don't *talk*! I don't do *anything*—I just mirror them back to *themselves*. People can't *see* themselves, so you *hold* up the glass, the mirror—no arguments, no resistance . . . I'm just a little *enzyme* that helps it all along, you see?

(Carol is looking blankly at Jerry.)

CAROL: And for this you charge two-fifty a session?
JERRY: The money is a guarantor of the *purity*, to not accept *money* darling that would just be errr *confusing* //
CAROL *(Sarcastic nodding)*: Keep going maestro //
JERRY: (and I *have* a sliding scale Carol // I'm not)
CAROL: Well get your sliding scale Jerry and let's slide back to the Upper East Side it's getting late *(Looks at her watch)* I need the check //

(Carol begins to retrieve her things, looks around for the waiter. Notices her ring is missing—looks around for it—)

JUDY: *No*, it's your anni*ver*sary We're taking *you* // out!
CAROL: Where's my ring?
JUDY: Oh—I forgot I was holding it.

(She takes it off and extends it to Carol. Martin intercedes and takes the ring.
He doesn't seem to be playing. Beat.)

CAROL: Can I have that.

(He looks at her.)

MARTIN: Why.
CAROL: Come on stop playing around.
MARTIN *(Looks at her)*: Do you know that you're full of *shit.*

[STOP]

CAROL: Stop playing // around.
MARTIN: I'm not playing around.

(Beat.)

CAROL: Can I have my ring please.
JUDY: Martin //
MARTIN: Shut up //
CAROL: Don't tell her to shut up.
JUDY: He's burnt // out
MARTIN: I TOLD YOU TO SHUT UP.

[STOP]

CAROL: Can // I
MARTIN: Take it, here.

> *(He hands her the ring.
> Pause.)*

You know what Judy?
You're that grit.
Not the pearl.
You're that unformed *thing*. That's what you are.

> *(Judy turns slowly to him.)*

JUDY *(Starting to shake)*: OK.

MARTIN *(Brutal)*: IT'S NOT OK.

(Beat.)

CAROL: Martin, you're acting insane.
JUDY: I'm sorry // if I
MARTIN: I was promised a pearl and I got grit; now it's time for the *shucking*.
JUDY: We were having such a nice time.
MARTIN: Am I invisible to you? Judy? Am I having a nice time?
JUDY: Honey you're scaring me.
MARTIN: you think I'm going to hit you? Maybe I should— because it's what you want, and I don't want to disappoint you being that we're all in *love* and we're *married* and we're little strumming *lovebirds*, with honey just *dripping* off our beaks, RIGHT?

[STOP]

Because you're obviously a *masochist* Judy, so *why* do *(He shakes her once)* I try to make things equal when I *love* you *so* much and I deny you—with all this *love*—your truest deepest wish? *(Beat)* Why should I deny you Judy when I pledged my *life* to you? How could I do that?
JUDY *(Hysterical)*: W-why why are y-you . . .

(Martin leaves.)

JERRY *(Drunk)*: Remember Martin: squash next Monday!
JUDY *(Shaking uncontrollably)*: Oh no.
CAROL *(Afraid to cause a scene)*: It's all right, Judy—just //
JUDY *(Having trouble breathing)*: "I believe."
CAROL: Are you . . .
JUDY *(Presses her hands to her temples, trying to quell the hysteria)*: I believe
I believe
I believe I believe I believe I bel—

(Loud music. We hear the chords, something punk, a wall of music, it cuts them off.)

[TITLE: "The Evildoers"]

(The space starts to transform; the chaos of the argument is parlayed into the transition. This should all have the tenor of ecstatic ritual—the seams of the play are starting to pull.
Jerry and Carol frantically undress and get into night-clothes.
Judy walks offstage in tears.
Martin grabs a raincoat and puts it on.
Thunder over music. Rain.
Martin fetches a bucket of ice for champagne. He pours it over his head.
Blackout.
The title cuts off and music cuts out into a five-second shockingly loud sample of a train speeding dangerously. This should feel rather jerky and unstable.)

[TITLE: "Strangers on a Train"]

(The lights snap on.)

2.

Three in the morning. A week later.
Carol and Martin are standing at the door of the Thernstroms' apartment. Martin is sopping wet, removing his coat. There's a frantic nervous energy.

MARTIN: I *know* it's late I'm *sorry* // I
CAROL: It's fine Martin Are you kidding We were *worried* about you // are you
MARTIN: It's so late it's—what, I don't // have my

CAROL: Three //

MARTIN *(Guilt)*: *Three!?* //

CAROL: No It's FINE I was up I was cleaning the oven //

MARTIN: I'm // so

CAROL: Let me get your— Look at you you're all // wet

MARTIN: Well //

CAROL: Do you think you have a fever?

MARTIN: No—

CAROL: How can you tell?

MARTIN: I just //

(He feels his head—she jerks his hand away, quickly feels his head.)

CAROL: (I don't think you have a fever) Sit DOWN (you need to rest) let me get you a blanket //

MARTIN *(Starts to move)*: Alright //

CAROL: *Don't track mud!* //

MARTIN: Uh //

CAROL: We just had the floors waxed (hold on) *no actually*: (I'm sorry // could)

MARTIN: Oh—

CAROL: you just take your shoes off there's a shoe rack, right // over—

MARTIN *(Flips off shoes)*: Sorry I'll clean // that

CAROL: No. NO Stop apologizing no it's just //

MARTIN: Uh. //

CAROL: We just we had the floors—well never mind, there's a blanket *(She gestures)* yeah put that on. *(He does—he looks rather pitiable)* Do you want something to drink?

MARTIN: No I'm all set, thanks.

[STOP]

CAROL: We have Coquilles St. Jacques from Fauchon I could reheat it.

MARTIN: Oh, no I'm not // hungry but

CAROL: You sure?

MARTIN: Yeah my stomach // feels

CAROL: (Do you want tums?) never // mind

MARTIN: I'm all set, Carol but thank you.

CAROL: Well. Anyway.

(Pause. Carol takes a pastille, sucks on it. They look out.)

That's a fake Franz Kline you like it?

JERRY *(Offstage)*: "Maaaartin?"

(Jerry enters in his pajamas and slippers, holding a pipe. He's still drunk, and still charming.)

Martin old man! *(To Carol)* You didn't tell me Martin was here, when'd you *get* here?

MARTIN: I didn't mean to wake you Jerry //

JERRY: WAKE me, oh come on I have inSOMnia, (I have *dreadful* insomnia) HEY you know you missed the squash game!

MARTIN: I'm sorry—

JERRY *(Pouts)*: I reserved the court and everything!

MARTIN: I know.

JERRY: Well I'm just glad you're OK.

MARTIN: Well thanks old man, I'm alright.

JERRY: "Old man"—you know I AM an old man Martin: I found a gray hair! and not on my head, NOOOOOOO, you know where you get

(Jerry opens a couple of buttons on his pajama top.)

them first? look, you see right on the aureole, abutting the NIPPLE, you see?

MARTIN: Uh—

JERRY: You see that: now what do you make of THAT? *(He sighs)* Well anyways . . . *(He closes his shirt and a button pops off)* Oh, uh—will you sew this on darling.

CAROL: No //

JERRY: JESUS CHRIST—

(He slips on the floor, nearly—but doesn't fall. He drops his pipe.)

CAROL: We had the floors waxed.

JERRY: Oh the damn floors that's right—oh my GOD— wow—where's my pipe?

(Martin finds it, hands it to him.)

CAROL: Do you have to smoke?

(Jerry lights up over the following:)

JERRY *(Smiling tensely)*: Darling, don't you want to go and put on some makeup or something.

CAROL: No.

MARTIN: I'm sorry, I—I feel // like I'm—

CAROL: Where's my virginia slims?

(She roots around for them.)

JERRY *(Puffs away)*: This is just like a *slumber* party.

CAROL: Isn't it.

JERRY: What are you looking for darling.

CAROL: My cigarettes, have you seen them?

JERRY *(To Martin)*: Carol thinks I look very "hung" in these pajamas.

(He looks down, puffing on his pipe, maybe snaps the waistband of his pajama bottoms.)

CAROL *(To Martin)*: Have you spoken to Judy?

MARTIN: Well //

JERRY: Judy's fine //

CAROL: No she ISN'T fine, you know she // isn't.

JERRY: Don't you worry about Judy, Martin.

CAROL: She's on medication.

JERRY: She's doing much // better.

CAROL: She's taking fistfuls of pills, she had a breakdown, she was in bad shape, she isn't FINE.

MARTIN: What do you // mean she

JERRY *(To Carol)*: She did not have a "breakdown," darling // she's

CAROL: Well that's what the doctor said.

JERRY: Well he's a hack, he wouldn't know a breakdown if he had one right in the goddamn mirror brushing his teeth // in the morning

CAROL *(To Martin)*: I told her she could stay with us, but she insisted on—anyway it's a big mess—but you're back, and it's fine—why don't you just call her.

MARTIN: I don't want to wake her.

CAROL: She's so distraught, Martin, really.

MARTIN: I don't really want to speak with her yet.

CAROL: But I think //

JERRY: He doesn't want to Carol.

CAROL: Why wouldn't he want to?

JERRY: Carol //

CAROL: I mean what are you doing at our door at three in the morning—I mean it's FINE, you have carte fucking *blanche*. Come here whenever you *want.*

MARTIN: Well I appreciate that.

CAROL: So are you having an affair, what? You're breaking up with // Judy?

JERRY: He's not having an // affair—

CAROL: Why, how do you know, are you two // colluding?

JERRY *(Disquisitive; holding forth)*: Listen: Carol: the male *animal* is designed for adventure—he lusts, he is a creature

of lust: this is the *quid pro quo* of the male animal, it's
what men DO. It's in our DNA, that's just what we do—

CAROL: No you don't walk out on your wife to have some
DNA-sequenced *adventure.*

MARTIN: That isn't it.

CAROL: And don't think I've forgotten what you said to Judy,
how you called her grit, and you acted all fucking insane
that night.

MARTIN: I apologized to Judy.

CAROL: She never mentioned that.

MARTIN: I apologized. I went through the ministrations of
guilt; that night, after we got back.

CAROL: Well then.

MARTIN: And Judy felt better. And we went to bed. And Judy
was sleeping next to me, she was in her little *fetal* position, with her little *toes* //

JERRY *(Sweet)*: Awww //

MARTIN: *Digging* into me //

JERRY *(Awkward)*: Oh—

MARTIN: and I couldn't sleep, I was still up*set*, something
was *gnawing* at me and I thought: you know what, fuck
this Judy, *I can't sleep*—I just thought I'd be gone a few
hours—I got on the Metro North, I thought I'll take it a
few stops, but then I just kept going . . . I got into the city
and I just sort of . . . rode around. And this guy came on
the subway and he sat across from me—he was staring at
me, it was making me uncomfortable. And I didn't feel
like getting up, so I thought, fine I'll stare him down.

(Beat.)

So I stared back.

(Beat.)

And then he did something very interesting.

(Beat.)

He reached down
into his pocket
and as he was reaching
he was looking
right at me, as if to . . . indicate . . . that this
reaching was
directed *towards* . . . me.

JERRY: In his pocket.

MARTIN: Yes. That somehow at the end of this seemingly enormous pocket was . . . me.

(Beat.)

JERRY: Why would he indicate to you that you were in his pocket?

CAROL: Sweetheart he was jerking off.

JERRY: *Oh.* Oh I *see.*

CAROL: I know all about this, it happens to girls all the time, men are always jerking off at you.

JERRY: On the subway? //

CAROL: (Well I take taxis) //

MARTIN: And then one thing led to another and . . . we were *kiss*ing.

JERRY: Were what?

MARTIN: Kissing. *(Beat)* French kissing.

JERRY: *French* kissing?

MARTIN: It's something I always wanted to try . . . with . . . with another . . .

CAROL *(Confounded)*: Why would you want to try THAT.

MARTIN: Because I. What do you mean "why"—I was curious.

(Beat.)

CAROL: Was your curiosity *satisfied?*

MARTIN *(Defensive)*: No; it wasn't.

(Short pause.)

CAROL: Meaning //
MARTIN: What do you think.

(Pause.)

I should go.

(He doesn't move.)

JERRY: Do you want another blanket, old man?
MARTIN: I'm warm now.

(Beat.)

CAROL: So are you *gay* // or
MARTIN *(A retaliation)*: Yes!

(Silence.)

CAROL: Why did you lie.
MARTIN: I don't want to talk about it.
JERRY *(Looks at Carol)*: You don't have to.

(Pause.)

MARTIN: It's stupid to feel ashamed, I know that, but I can't
help it.

(Pause.)

CAROL: So you're leaving Judy? This is the *sine qua non* right?
MARTIN *(Quiet)*: Yeah.

CAROL (*No emotion*): That's sad.

[STOP]

(*Fillip of anger*) Don't you care about what happens to
Judy?
JERRY: Carol:

(*Silence.*)

MARTIN (*Very vulnerable here*): He's an architect. He took me
back to his brownstone. His wife was at a conference,
but she came back today and I had to go. They have an
understanding. (*Suddenly, irrationally heartbroken*) So
we can't be involved in an emotional way, just physical.

(*Pause.
He looks up at them, his eyes brimming with tears.*)

But I need more.

(*Snap blackout.*)

3.

*Later the same night. Martin is set up with a blanket and sheets
on the sofa. He's reading Updike's* Couples *against the glow of
very soft lamplight.
Jerry sneakily enters, unseen by Martin.
He tiptoes drunkenly, until he's right behind Martin.*

JERRY: *Comfy?*
MARTIN: Jesus you—
JERRY: Heh heh heh heh.
MARTIN: You scared me.

JERRY: You want another blanket something with a higher *threadcount* maybe. Carol's BIG on "threadcount."

MARTIN: I'm OK.

(Jerry takes Martin's book from him. Looks at the cover.)

JERRY *(Sloshed)*: Updike. Up-dike.

(Beat.)

He's prolific but that's not tantamount to good. That's not tantamount to SHIT. *(Beat)* I don't even know what tantamount *means*, I just *say* these things, they *issue forth* from my lips and I KNOW that they're true, I have an instinct. And we can't dismiss our instincts, don't you agree, because it would be catastrophic—I mean the effect of that, of. *(Beat)* And you can accept me can't you Martin, with my flaws, my foibles, my little peccadilloes, my little . . . my *things*; can't you?

MARTIN: Of course Jer.

JERRY: *HEY*—I really feel like a RÉMY you'd like a Rémy wouldn't you alright so I'll SIDLE up to the bar and— GET ONE—how's that I'll just—

(He tries to get up—stumbles.)

MARTIN: Jerry why don't you sit down //

JERRY: Am I keeping you up old man, I //

MARTIN *(Going over to the bar)*: You sit *down* and *I'll* get you a drink.

JERRY: Oh, yay, (well you really don't have to) I mean if you're sleepy, I really don't want to trouble you, you're a guest in our home.

MARTIN: It's fine Jer.

JERRY: Well that's kind of you Martin.

(He watches Martin prepare a drink.)

"Jer" I like that, the shorthand "Jer" but that's what friends are they're people who know each other's minds,

MARTIN: You like it neat right //

JERRY: and they speak in shorthand, glyphs, there's all kinds of—what //

MARTIN: You //

JERRY: That's perfect, that's just how I like it. Thank you Martin.

(Beat.)

She's a darling girl isn't she?

MARTIN: Who?

JERRY: Carol!

MARTIN: Oh.

JERRY: Don't you think?

MARTIN: Sure.

JERRY: And—you know; because we're having a *baby* and everything.

(Beat.)

MARTIN: She's *pregnant?*

JERRY: What? Oh, er—YES—oh you didn't //

MARTIN: When did THIS happen?

JERRY: I thought I //

MARTIN: Congratulations old man!

JERRY: My "issue," yes— You know what Freud says about babies—he compares *babies* you see to *feces*, it's rather wacky, but he—means it in a good way, he's very—People misunderSTAND Freud, he's just a nice— (oh that's it for me, thanks old man, that's) —ha ha—oh swell.

(Holds up his glass.)

"To my little feces!"

MARTIN *(Laughing)*: Here here.

JERRY: HA HA HA "my feces"
HA HA HA
Oh
"Oy vey"
HA HA HA
(Wiping tears from his eyes)
oh my goodness-I so-love-Freud
(Sips drink)
its—it's *pathological*

(Beat.)

MARTIN: When's she due //
JERRY: I think the fall sometime.
MARTIN: It's fall now.
JERRY: OH: oh I mean next fall.
MARTIN *(After a beat)*: But, then she'd be pregnant for a *year.*
JERRY: Oh; well I-I-I *spring* or something //

(Jerry sips his drink.)

Carol's a lovely girl really. *(Pause)* I mean it's not all roses, she complains, she has complaints.
MARTIN: About?
JERRY: You know: well for instance about my sperm and everything: she says it's too *chunky*—I mean al*right*, it's not so well blended, but I eat avocados!!—I don't know, something happened to me. But HEY: the stuff works, chunky, smooth, who's complaining!

(Slaps him in the back. Beat. Sips drink.)

MARTIN *(Excitedly)*: Jerry: you're going to be a DADDY.
JERRY *(Weird baby voice)*: "da da" heheheh //
MARTIN: How do you *feel?*
JERRY: Feel? *(Thinks about it)* well I feel—frightened.

MARTIN: Why?

JERRY: Well

I'm not sure.

I feel OK right now Martin, with you here, I'm not frightened at this very moment.

MARTIN: Neither am I //

JERRY *(Screams)*: BOO!

MARTIN *(Recoiling in shock)*: AH!

JERRY: HAHAHAH //

MARTIN: HAHAHHAH //

JERRY *(Loud whisper)*: Shhh (ha ha ha) shh let's—ho ho— let's not wake Carol.

MARTIN: All right.

(Another button on Jerry's pajama top has fallen off.)

JERRY *(Pouty)*: Oh, now the other, oh, the *button*, now I'll really have to—and these are my *best pair* of pajamas, they're my favorite, my favorite in the whole world . . .

(Beat.)

MARTIN: Nice nips Jer.

JERRY: Well thanks old man I like them too. Carol doesn't think they're—

(Martin lunges for Jerry's nipple and tweaks it.)

OW!

(Martin jumps up, runs, trying to stifle his laughter.)

You *bastard.*

(Martin laughs. Jerry tries to go after Martin and slips— benignly—on the waxed floor.)

(Pointing, laughing) You're a dead man. *(Getting himself up again)* Oh these damn FLOORS.

MARTIN: This is just like boarding school all over again! //

JERRY: *Isn't* // it?

MARTIN: Remember when Phil waxed your ass // in the

JERRY: reMEMber? Martin, I felt that in the back of my *throat* for god's sake.

(They laugh.)

Oh, my salad days, what happened?

MARTIN *(After a beat)*: They wilted.

JERRY *(Tickled)*: Wilted? Oh SHIT—

MARTIN: Ha ha.

JERRY *(Hits him)*: Don't shit me!

MARTIN: Ow.

JERRY: Oh—er—

MARTIN: Ha ha ha ha.

(Jerry laughs.)

JERRY: You'll always have me Martin, you know that; I mean I don't care if you fuck *light fixtures*. Or. (well-that-sounds-like-a-bad-joke-but-//-you)

MARTIN: Thanks Jerry

JERRY: You keep looking up at the chandelier, I mean—fuck it if you want, fuck the bookshelf! Just don't spooj on my Freud seminars other than that ha ha ha HAHA. *(Beat, then very sweetly, intimate)* I'm your friend. Alright? Truly. *(Clutches his hand)* Truly and profoundly. *(Pause)* And drunkenly.

(Martin removes his hand, smiles awkwardly.
Long silence.
Martin pulls an argyle sock from his pant's pocket.
Pause.)

MARTIN: Look.

(Jerry regards the sock. A pause.)

JERRY: Is—that for me?

(Long pause.)

MARTIN: I took it.

(Silence.)

I'm pathetic, I took it from his—drawer.

(Beat.)

JERRY *(Drunk)*: I need socks. My sock has a hole in it.

(Long pause.)

MARTIN: He . . . builds things?

(Tiny smile to cover.)

(Very tiny) There were these . . . *Models?* . . . everywhere?

(He looks at Jerry; a deep sadness, a plaintiveness un-earthed.)

JERRY: What's the matter old boy?

(Pause.)

MARTIN: I'm forty—I'm almost *forty*, my life is halfway done, and there's nothing *in it.* And it's too late for me // now
JERRY: It's not // too

MARTIN *(Coming apart here)*: *Why* am I stealing socks from people's drawers, it's so—*stupid*—I'm *stupid*, I—I feel so— And I shouldn't I shouldn't feel this way— It's wrong to feel ashamed, it's *wrong*, but it's *embedded* in me, so deep, it's *lodged* in me—that's why I'm *stunted.* My feelings are—*stunted*—I—at work I walk around— in the cafeteria, everyone's smiling, they're—and I don't know what to do with my *hands*, I don't know how to stand—I'm *numb*—

JERRY: Shhh—now come on //

MARTIN: There are h-h- people—in the world—like *me*— they aren't crippled by—they have some kind of joy, they let themselves but I can't, why?

JERRY: Well, you've always been a little wound up.

MARTIN: I'm so fucked up . . . and Judy's so fucked up—and I can't just *leave* her like this—she can't take care of herself . . .

(He looks at Jerry, so deeply sad.)

JERRY: It's—its all going to—work out.

(Martin rises, wipes his tears quickly, decisively, starts to dress.)

MARTIN: I'm gonna go //

JERRY: Now? // er—

MARTIN: I'm gonna go back. // Maybe she'll

JERRY: You're getting all—riled up here old man— *(Grabs his arm)* just—now hold *on* // here a minute—

MARTIN *(Throws him off)*: DON'T TELL ME TO HOLD ON—

(Jerry looks at him. A pause. Quiet.)

Oh my god I'm being completely crazy. Jerry I'm sorry— I'm // so sorry.

JERRY: It's—fine old man, it's—fine—now:

MARTIN: What's wrong with me.

JERRY: You've had a rough week. Now why don't you have a seat on the old sofa? Hmmm? *(He pats it, smiles gingerly)* Nice and comfy, all for you Martin *(He pats it a few more times. Martin reluctantly sits)*

(Long pause.)

MARTIN: I made a mistake. *(Nods sadly)* I can't just leave her like this. // This is—

JERRY *(Perfectly sanguine)*: Everything is going to be just *fine* //

MARTIN: I'm being // *crazy*

JERRY: Judy is going to be *fine*.

(A beat.)

(Smiling, encouraging) Judy's like a little rubber *band* Martin She'll just "snap back" into place.

MARTIN: That isn't true.

(Beat. Smile fades.)

JERRY: Well maybe it isn't true. *(Beat)* But you're not doing her a favor by *deferring* the pain, are you?

(Beat.)

Listen old man you're HELPING Judy. I mean yes she's suffering and it's hard—but suffering can be *good* for a person, you know, it's quite *tonic*, suffering.

MARTIN: How is it good?

JERRY: Well the pain, you know *(Beat)* it's *cleansing*—it's like in the Bible you see, when Jesus, or someone, I think it was him, he says "suffer little children"—remember that?

[STOP]

Well he does. Because the suffering is *good, that's* why he says it, it's *cleansing*, it strips you down and—it's like those Russian dolls.

MARTIN: What dolls?

JERRY: You know those *(Gestures)* you just keep removing the big ones until you get to the littlest doll, and that's the densest, best one, the little doll in the middle, it's like a little *nugget*—a nugget of *truth. (Beat) Don't look at me like that*, I have a lot of good ideas!—I'm making a lot of *sense* here: now look: the pain, see, that helps you to strip it down, and you just strip strip strip—strip the whole business down, that's the thing about suffering, it breaks you *down* and it breaks you into *pieces*: and it's absolutely: *dem*ocratic: it's a *democracy*. And then you become your authentic self, and you're a whole SELF! Like one of those dolls, like—a little errrr *crystal* of yourself. Now, don't you want that for Judy?

(Martin nods.)

And don't you want it for your*self*? *(Martin looks at him)* You're on the path now Martin.

MARTIN *(A beat)*: Am I?

JERRY: Listen, pain is just the beginning—it's the opening, you have to get inside the wound . . . don't you see? *(Beat)* this is the *path*.

(Pause.)

MARTIN: Really?

JERRY: YES, you're figuring it all out now, just keep going. *(Waves his hand along)*

MARTIN: But //

JERRY: Keep going! Do it for Judy, do it for Carol—for me! You're helping *everyone*!

MARTIN: How?

(Beat. Jerry thinks about it a second.)

JERRY: It's a ripple effect! "Suffer little children"—suffering makes you human.

MARTIN: It does?

JERRY: Oh yes, yes. Let me tell you something about Human, these *people*, no one knows what human is, because it's not what you think. *(Beat)* You know what Christ says? "Love thine enemy."

MARTIN: Yeah

JERRY: Not your neighbor, but your *enemy*. You know why he says that?

MARTIN: Why?

(Jerry leans in.)

JERRY: It's a *code*. *(Smiles and nods his head, eyebrows raised)* It's a very deep, *gnomic* thing you see. You can't love your enemy—it's a *non*sensical—you know—it makes no *sense*, you can't love someone you don't love—because you *hate them*! I mean that's a doomed enterprise don't you think? so why does he *say it*—and then he actually enjoins you to do it!

MARTIN: Is it because—that love is—that we're meant to // suffer?

JERRY: It's that *love*—ergo *human*—can't be what we *think*. *(Beat) Real* love. *Christian* love. It's not about feelings— *feeling* love. It's deeper.

MARTIN: Like the Russian doll?

(Jerry weaves drunkenly.)

JERRY: Wha?

MARTIN: The—Russian // doll?

JERRY: Listen—Martin, you know these—subatomic *particles*?

MARTIN: What?

JERRY: Subatomic—you know—the—the //

MARTIN: You mean like—quarks?

JERRY: *Quarks*—yes! It's like *quarks*! I mean *quarks*—think about it, do they *dislike* other quarks? They don't have *enemies*— They don't have love, they just sit around being quarks and composing matter. Does a quark say, "I don't like that quark, I'm going to kill it, I'm going to rape it, I'm unhappy, I want a divorce." NO. because these things aren't real. And what could be MORE real than quarks? I mean—we fucking ARE quarks—that's how REAL they are, without quarks there could BE no human beings . . . do you see?

(Pause.)

MARTIN: So: Christ wants us to be like—*quarks?*

JERRY *(Shakes his head no—wobbling)*: We ARE the quarks old man . . .

(Martin looks at him.)

MARTIN *(Tentative)*: I'm quarks.

JERRY: The *fundaments*!

(Martin looks at him.)

MARTIN: We're quarks.

JERRY: That's right.

MARTIN: And Christ . . . *wants* us to . . . *be* quarks—to *know* we're quarks //

JERRY *(Nods excitedly)*: Keep going!

MARTIN: But we don't *know* we're the quarks because //

JERRY: Yeeesss?

MARTIN: because—we think we're the Russian—*dolls!*—not the little one in the middle—the big clunky one on the *outside*. But—that doll's a lie! Right? We're not that doll . . .

(Pause.)

JERRY *(Drunk)*: The *Wha?*

MARTIN: Because—that's not the *human* . . .

JERRY *(Sips)*: Wha human?

MARTIN: And that's how you love your *Enemy*! by getting to that—*place*—inside the *molecules* //

JERRY *(Plastered beyond measure)*: Strip-strip-strip!

MARTIN: and to do that . . . you have to enter their suffering . . . or else *you* suffer. *(A discovery)* Because it's all linked up. *(Pause)* It's *one* thing.

(Pause.)

JERRY: "Suffer little children . . ."

(Beat.)

only in that case it doesn't mean "suffer"—I just remembered—it means something like "get over here."

MARTIN *(Mock anger)*: "Get over here"!

(They laugh.)

JERRY: And when I was a runner, remember in high school Martin and I was running on that running team remember I would—I mean *god* knows—I mean—FUCK—I killed myself, sprinting, running, jumping I don't know what the fuck I // was HA HA

MARTIN: You were good too.

JERRY: I was, I was very fleet //

MARTIN: You were fast.

JERRY: And the pain in my calves every morning and *(Beat)* and you know I *miss* that . . . without that *pain* there's— you know, you feel deprived . . . your life is . . . empty.

(Martin studies him very intently.)

MARTIN: Is that how you feel?

JERRY *(Snapping out of it)*: What? No. NO no.
ha ha ha.
(He drinks; Martin is staring at him)
Is something . . . the matter?

MARTIN *(Beat)*: God, it's almost six I should try and get some sleep.

JERRY: Well—I won't keep you up with any more of my blather.

MARTIN: You're not keeping me up.

(Martin looks in his eyes. Then looks away, discomfited.)

JERRY: Martin?

(Pause.)

What is it?

MARTIN: Oh . . . nothing.

JERRY: What is it old man?

(Beat.)

MARTIN: You'll think I'm crazy.

JERRY: I won't think you're crazy.

(Pause.)

MARTIN: Well. I just. I think I went "inside the molecules."

(Beat.)

JERRY: You did NOT.

(Martin nods. Jerry looks at him.)

What happened?

(Beat.)

MARTIN: You seemed very . . . sad . . . to me . . .
JERRY: *Sad?*

(Pause.)

But—I'm alright—I'm not *sad*, I feel fine, in fact I'm in
a very jocular MOOD.
MARTIN: No?—well all right, that's
JERRY: I *feel* fine . . . But you're saying I'm—sad . . .
MARTIN: It's all right—I think I'm going a little—*nuts* over
here, it's been a long—

(He accidentally spills Jerry's drink.)

SHIT—I'll clean that—

(Jerry gets up—Martin stands, helps him.)

JERRY: There's nothing wrong.
MARTIN: Is there a—do you have a rag or, or a //
JERRY *(Smiling, drunk)*: There's nothing wrong with me.
Alright? If I were unhappy somehow if I were unhappy
I would tell you, of course I would, you're my friend.
You're my dear *friend.*

*(Martin nods, looks away.
Martin starts sobbing.
Jerry looks at him, sadly.)*

(Consolingly) Everything is OK.

*(Martin turns to him; he forces a tiny sympathetic smile.
He touches Jerry's hair.
He holds Jerry's face in his hand, with real love, and real
empathy.*

He—and it's sudden—kisses Jerry fully on the mouth.
Jerry acquiesces briefly—then pulls away . . .)

Oh.
Whoo.
(Beat. He smiles, musingly)
Gee. *(Beat. Amused)*
What do you think *that* was?

(He laughs. He ribs Martin. Martin doesn't crack a smile,
he seems worried. He looks away from Jerry.
The sound of the train and whistle comes up and gets
unbearably loud. Lights snap off; sound cuts out.)

Act Two

1.

Judy and Martin's home in Fleetwood. The apartment is lit with candles.
Things are still in boxes, in neat stacks. Some of the boxes are opened, some not.
Carol is munching on dried apricots, chain smoking virginia slims, reading to Judy from Huxley's Brave New World.
Judy's hair has a shock of white in it.

CAROL: "... and oh, oh at my breast, the little hands, the hunger, and that unspeakable, agonizing pleasure! Till at last my baby sleeps, my baby sleeps with a bubble of white milk at the corner of his mouth. My little baby sleeps." *(Beat. Looks up)* This is a rather reactionary little book isn't it. *(Slams the book shut)*
JUDY: Keep reading //

(Carol lights a cigarette.)

CAROL: But I've already read eight pages Judy and the type-face is so small //

JUDY: I haven't been read to in ages //

CAROL: Get books on tape, I find Alan Alda's tenor so soothing //

JUDY: *Goodnight Moon* //

CAROL: Martin got these for me, I don't know why, they're good, they're spiced with something //

JUDY: My father used to read to me

CAROL (*Munching on an apricot*): He's behaving rather strangely, him and Jerry, you should see them poring over *Bibles* it's driving me up a wall //

JUDY: *Goodnight Moon.*

CAROL: What?

JUDY: It's a book

CAROL: What is it some nuclear holocaust thing?

JUDY: (What) //

CAROL: It's so *country* up here. (*Holds out bag of apricots*) Want some apricots.

JUDY: When do you give birth //

CAROL: I like your hair by the way.

JUDY: You should read it to the baby, I used to love that book.

CAROL: (Oh right I have to read it things) //

JUDY: When are you due?

CAROL: June something // it's in

JUDY: June—

CAROL: my palm pilot

(*Beat.*)

JUDY: Do you want something to drink.

CAROL: You know I really like this hair thing, the shock of white, very Sontag.

JUDY: But she's dead.

CAROL: But you're immortalizing her *hair*.

JUDY (*Regarding Carol's cigarette*): Could you—

CAROL (*Puffing manically*): A few more puffs.

JUDY: You're pregnant?

CAROL: Yeah I don't know *(Puff)* my mother smoked like a chimney when she had me. *(Puff)* there was a lot of traffic getting here I was surprised. *(Beat)* So what are you going to do?

JUDY: What am I //

CAROL: Are you going to sell this place, or //

JUDY: I don't know.

(Pause.)

CAROL *(Brightly)*: I have a friend who builds tract housing for millionaires he's lovely. He's the great-grandnephew of Gustav Klimt or something unbelievable like that, isn't that so snarky no but he's great, he's got these gorgeous eyelashes, I think he's gay, oh he's so annoying, why's everyone gay. *(Oops—a gaffe. Beat. Then brightly again)* But I like what you've done with the place—kind of. (Well. the candles, I don't know) I mean—its *nice* and everything but it's a bit goth for me.

JUDY: The electricity's not working.

CAROL: What's the problem.

JUDY: The wiring?

CAROL: Did you call the electrician?

JUDY: He said not to touch it, there was a blackout //

CAROL: Who?

JUDY *(Tiny stutter)*: M-Martin was supposed // to

CAROL: Well call the electrician.

JUDY: It's fine.

CAROL: Is that *all* anyone ever says anymore, "It's *fine*"?

JUDY *(Unfocused)*: He was kidnapped, it's a whole story and I don't have the patience to do anything about it just now

CAROL: The electrician was kidnapped?

JUDY: No, his daughter.

CAROL: How dreadful.

JUDY: Could you read some more, it was soothing.

CAROL: I could find you someone, I know electricians I think.
JUDY: I'm capable, I can find one.
CAROL: You're sure?
JUDY: This is teakwood isn't it lovely?

(Carol sees a book on the table. She opens it.)

I started that in the hospital,
CAROL: What is it, some kind of art project?
JUDY: It's just pictures.

(Carol opens it. She turns a few pages. She's aghast.)

I've been looking at articles and things, I'm very—

(Pause.)

I've been reading about Pol Pot, and about the Kurds?
and—just all these . . . these political things, and I find
it very compelling.
CAROL: It's a little—disturbing.
JUDY: Well. We all have to see disturbing things sometimes.

*(Carol flips through the book—slowly—registering shock.
She looks at Judy.)*

CAROL: Your doctor's seen this?

(Judy spontaneously begins to weep.)

JUDY: Now I—I feel ashamed.
CAROL: Why are you crying.
JUDY *(Covering)*: Could I have that back?
CAROL: I think it's good you—have *pro*jects; I'm not saying
feel *ashamed*—
JUDY: I'm not ashamed, it's—the light hurts my eyes.

CAROL *(Referring to the lack of light)*: *What* light?

JUDY: And I'm not crying // I'm

CAROL: Judy you can't live without electricity, this is // ridiculous

JUDY: I don't want to argue //

CAROL: We're not arguing //

JUDY *(Vulnerably)*: No—no because we *love* each other.

CAROL *(Flip)*: I don't know about that, I'm just saying we're not arguing. HA HA HA I'm TEASING sweetheart.

(Judy says nothing—she hasn't the mettle.)

(More gently) Maybe you should stay with your mother.

JUDY: No—she doesn't want me.

CAROL: Don't be martyry of course she *wants* you.

(Judy says nothing.)

(Very gingerly) I just think being up here like this, it's a bit . . . too . . . *monastic*; you need to be around other *people*.

(Judy looks at Carol, tentative.)

JUDY: The doctor? At the hospital? He said that I needed to *pretend* I had one good parent, that's what people do. But that my parents were both very—abusive //

CAROL: "Abusive"?

JUDY: To me? That's what he told me, we discussed it. He said people like to believe that they have one good parent, to feel safe, but it's not true.

CAROL: That sounds like forgive me but a bunch of claptrap //

JUDY *(Pleading)*: And that that's why I married, I—I'm-m-m, that's why I got m-married? You know?

CAROL: Well I like your mother a tremendous lot, she has character // ("abusive," that's

JUDY: "Character."

CAROL: such textbook Freudian bullcrap.) //

JUDY: She //

CAROL: Mothers love their children, that's innate, it's a physiological thing (I mean yeah *some* of them drown their kids but) // that's—

JUDY: Well //

CAROL: Do you want an apricot? //

JUDY: that's what he. He told me my // parents were

CAROL: I'm not saying she's perfect, I'm saying she doesn't know any better, her parents were immigrants.

JUDY: (They weren't immigrants.)

CAROL: Well-she-speaks-with-that-accent //

JUDY: (No // she)

CAROL *(Impatient, rancor)*: Well WHATEVER Judy—I'm just // saying

JUDY: I think—for right now? I should just be up here // and I

CAROL: Jerry said this guy was a hack, I don't think you should listen to him //

JUDY: Or—

CAROL: LISTEN: let's pack a few things, you'll come back with me in the hummer.

JUDY: I can't //

CAROL: Where's your suitcase //

JUDY: Could you please keep reading, you stopped and it was so *soothing* //

CAROL: We could go to La Goulue, they have that prix fixe, what time is it, I'll call your mum and we . . .

(Judy fearfully nods no.)

Do you like it here? how could you like it here?

JUDY *(Sad)*: I don't.

CAROL: No, you couldn't, because it's dreadful.

(Beat.)

JUDY *(Slow acknowledgment)*: It's . . . dreadful. Yes.
CAROL: Then come on—
JUDY: I . . . hate it here.
CAROL: Darling
JUDY: I hate my life. I don't know what I'm doing, oh my god //
CAROL: But then it'll all flip around,
JUDY: Oh my GOD Carol.
CAROL: you just have to change it.
JUDY: *How*, I *can't*—
CAROL: You just have to know what you want, but you're too fucked up for that just now, OK sweetheart?

(Judy absentmindedly opens her scrapbook.)

JUDY: Did you know that in China there's a group called "Falun Gong," and the Chinese government wedges like pieces of wood under their fingernails, they have these devices, they dig nails into—their—FACES //
CAROL: I don't want to talk about Falun Gong, let's just pack.
JUDY: And in Iran—
CAROL *(Abrupt; sarcasm)*: And you're *like* all these people, *right?* you *identify* with them?
JUDY: *No* //
CAROL: Because your husband is a fag and he walked out on you so you're a torture victim!
JUDY: I // didn't
CAROL: Because let me tell you something you have a fabulous fucking life, and if you lived under Mao or Pol Pot or whoever the fuck you'd be really fucking sorry, it's not comparable, do you understand—I know you're having a hard time but really you must try to not be so florid about your grief: divorce is completely ordinary; *most* people get divorced, you're the status *quo*—

JUDY: Yes.

CAROL: If Jerry left *me* I wouldn't *care*. because my identity isn't based on my marriage, my own health has really pretty little to do with the health of my *marriage*. Just because the marriage is falling apart doesn't mean that *I'm* going to fall apart; so don't fall into that trap.

(She holds up the scrapbook.)

This: is not *you*: do you understand—these feelings are not *your* feelings, don't feed on this bullshit, it's pathetic.

(She rips up the book.)

[STOP]

What, don't look at me like that.
Here have an apricot.

JUDY: He got them for you.

CAROL: What.

JUDY *(Near tears)*: He *got* them for YOU don't BRING them here.

(Beat.)

CAROL: Judy //

JUDY: You're *living* with him . . . you *see* him, do I want to KNOW about that?

CAROL: Well what do you want me to do // Judy

JUDY: Just put those away please.

CAROL: They're APRICOTS //

JUDY *(Shaken)*: PUT THEM AWAY.

(Carol puts the apricots in her bag—shuts it with a histrionic clang.)

CAROL: Remember that thing when you stood too near to that Chuck Close painting and that thing in your brain happened well *I'm having that now.*

[STOP]

JUDY: You're . . . just like her.

(Carol starts packing.)

CAROL: This is a cute top, where'd you get this, Barneys Co-Op?
JUDY: I don't know how I never saw it.
CAROL: (Saw what) I like the décolletage //
JUDY: You're like her . . . you're like my *mother.*
CAROL: Why because I'm *abusive*? Is mother code now for "abusive"? Did they do like reverse neuro-linguistic *pro*gramming on you // *Judy*?
JUDY: Please put that back, I'm not coming with you.

(Judy takes the sweater.)

CAROL: How am I abusive? *(Pulls the sweater back)* Oh, you're being unreasonable. And your mother loves you Judy she's just a little—*stalwart.*

(Carol resumes packing for her—then stops abruptly.)

JUDY: *She'd* come here, and *she'd* rip up my things //
CAROL: Come ON //
JUDY: and *she'd* drag me around, and force me to wear her horrible // scarves
CAROL: Judy //
JUDY: and she'd say it was because *she* loved me.
CAROL: She does love you.
JUDY: She can't stand me.
CAROL: Are you saying *I* can't stand me—*I mean YOU.*

JUDY: Put that back please.

CAROL: You're coming with // me—

JUDY: "Yes mother" //

CAROL: OK the mother thing is freaking me out—I'm starting to have second thoughts, maybe I should uh—ABORT?!? I mean—uh—ha ha—uh . . .

(Carol resumes packing.)

JUDY: Maybe you should.

(She turns to Judy, who's serious.)

CAROL: Well *thanks.*

JUDY *(Earnestly)*: I think that as a mother you'd be a catastrophe.

(Pause.
Carol laughs—thinking this is a joke. Oh—it's not a joke.)

CAROL: I have a meeting.

JUDY: Yes; go to your meeting.

(Pause.)

CAROL: I have to be back in the city.

(Carol looks at her, worriedly.)

Are you sure you . . .

(Judy looks out.
Carol hesitates, then gets her things. She exits.
Music in:
Judy smiles softly, a strange, sad smile, as the tears come.)

[TITLE: "The Fright of Real Tears"]

2.

The Thernstroms' apartment. Thanksgiving eve—Martin, Jerry and Carol are all having a traditional Thanksgiving dinner. Martin is wearing a pink oxford shirt, his hair is slicked back. It should all register as a little too proleptically "gay"— he's getting ahead of himself. The rhythms here should be fast and furious.

CAROL: Pass the yams //

MARTIN: And she and then // she

JERRY: And where were you?

MARTIN: I'm—

JERRY *(Remembering)*: (Yes yes yes yes yes) //

MARTIN: She ripped off a piece of the duct tape //

JERRY: The mother //

MARTIN: Uh-huh and she put it on the girl's mouth, and she ripped it off and the daughter had these tears—she had these // tears

CAROL: Pass the yams.

MARTIN: And the girl says I'm going to TELL them what you do to me and the mother says who's going to believe you who's going to believe YOU //

JERRY *(Pouring wine for Martin)*: You—

MARTIN: (No no) and the daughter. Uh. had these pink eyes it was //

JERRY: Well //

MARTIN: Do you know what that means?

CAROL: Jerry isn't wearing his secret decoder ring right now? so // I don't think

JERRY: Carol //

MARTIN: I'm sorry is this tedious I shouldn't be belaboring— I'm sure everyone comes to you with their dreams.

JERRY: Not Carol //

CAROL: Because I don't dream.

MARTIN: Everybody dreams.

JERRY: You don't REMEMBER // your dreams

CAROL *(To Jerry)*: (Stop picking your eyebrows) //

MARTIN: If you don't dream you go insane.

CAROL: Hence: my life. HA HA HA.

JERRY *(Squeezing her arm)*: Now // daarlling

CAROL: What, *no* (stop clawing me) don't // spill that

JERRY *(Sings quietly)*: "You made me me love // you"
  (da da da da da da
  do do do do . . .)

MARTIN: These brussel // sprouts are

CAROL: Oh you like those I got the recipe from Mario Batali
  it's—you roast them it's really easy.

JERRY: How are you feeling darling?

CAROL: I'm a little sick actually,

JERRY: Maybe you should //

CAROL *(To Martin)*: You know *yams* are a *superfood* //

MARTIN: Really

CAROL: they have lots of minerals, yams, they're superfoods,
  lots of vitamins and they're // so

MARTIN *(To Jerry)*: I guess //

CAROL: They're // so

MARTIN: I mean the idea of feeling stifled, that you won't be
  HEARD: that's part of it.

JERRY: Uh—

MARTIN: The dream?

JERRY: *Oh!*

MARTIN: And in a way it's like—and there was violence, and
  this kid //

CAROL: And cruciferous vegetables.

MARTIN: I'm sure—

JERRY *(To Carol)*: What's that dear?

CAROL: Cruciferous vegetables, those are superfoods.

JERRY: They're shaped like little crucifixes //

MARTIN *(Non sequitur)*: As a gay man, I mean *that's what's
  so* // *exhilarating*—

CAROL (*Noticing her ring is gone*): Where's //

MARTIN: that I'm—I'm not *that*—because that's what I've come to realize, that there's no silver bullet, that's the thing, no *shortcut*, that's the problem with. Or maybe there *is* a shortcut but if you *take* one you'll never get there, you have to enter the wound.

CAROL: Where's my //

JERRY: Did you say something darling?

CAROL: My ring, I had it right on my—you didn't do anything with //

JERRY: No darling no I // didn't—

CAROL: Well where is it WHERE IS IT?

JERRY: Well we'll find it we'll FIND //

MARTIN (*Finds it*): Bingo

JERRY: Darling here it is, here it is—

CAROL: Now how did that—

MARTIN: Right here //

CAROL: I took it off that's right, oh thank you Martin.

(*Pause.*)

MARTIN: It's so interesting Carol.

CAROL: What's that Martin.

MARTIN: This attachment you have to—well now it's a piece of costume jewelry but. Well it's not a part of your history anymore, you can see that can't you it's just a pretty *thing.*

CAROL (*Taut smile*): Well it really isn't and you're sweet but any of your business.

MARTIN: I'm just //

CAROL: So let's terminate the conversation now shall we. (*Beat*) and while we're at it you really aren't a paragon for marital happiness—

MARTIN (*Not ceding the ring*): No I'm not—

CAROL: Can I have that back?

(He holds the ring out to her; she puts it on.)

MARTIN: I'm just super sensitive right now, I'm sensitive to things because MY situation is so unstable.

CAROL: Well some systems tend toward entropy. *(Beat)* Speaking of which Martin what is your plan?

MARTIN: For . . .

CAROL: Your situation? do you have a plan? or //

MARTIN: A plan //

CAROL: For your life?

MARTIN *(After a beat)*: Well I'm still trying to . . . orient myself . . .

CAROL *(Beat)*: So your plan is to be *oriented?*

MARTIN *(Laughing)*: Well // no—

CAROL: No, that's legitimate, that's a legitimate goal, we all need to be oriented, I mean we can't go around smacking into walls, that's not a way to live. *(Beat)* Well good.

JERRY *(Picking out his eyebrows yet again)*: Martin's just— figuring it out right old man.

CAROL *(Pulling Jerry's hand away)*: STOP THAT //

JERRY: I'm not. They just fall out //

CAROL: (Your // *eye*brows)

JERRY *(Pouring more wine)*: I *know* Carol "the pillars of the face" I know but // I don't

MARTIN: And Carol I know I've hurt Judy, I'm *not* saying I'm a paragon // of

CAROL: No no no DON'T exculpate yourself here all right // let me tell

MARTIN: I'm not—

CAROL: you something you don't give a shit about Judy: you haven't seen her, you haven't talked anything through. And you're avoiding the situation you aren't being brave you aren't honest you're a coward So spare me the sanctimony.

(Pause.)

MARTIN *(Meaning it, or wanting to)*: Thank you. You're right.
I am a coward. Thank you Carol—I'm—inching towards //
my progress.

CAROL: And you have this CREEPY actually fixation on my
engagement ring I // mean

JERRY: I don't think it's creepy //

CAROL: Well it is //

MARTIN: I'm just trying to understand you, I'm trying to understand the kind of person you are.

CAROL *(Eating)*: And what kind of person is that.

*(She waits for a response. Martin does not respond. He
eats. She looks up at him.*
Carol laughs, pretending to be cavalier.)

You know I can see it now.

MARTIN: What.

CAROL *(Drops the smile)*: The Jewishness, you have that. Uh.
Hebraic severity. *(Beat)* And Jewish people like to repeat
things don't they, oh that's funny I see it now. *(She eats)*
The repetition—that's where that must come from—
it's that *Talmud* thing isn't it, the endless regurgitation.
You're. *(She chews)* So exhaustive.

(She eats. This is uncomfortable.)

MARTIN: You know Carol you're incredibly privileged: you're
having a *kid*, and you have a *marriage*, you—can I get
married? no //

CAROL: Go to Massachusetts //

MARTIN: And you have a LIFE—I have a "lifestyle"—I have
a "gay // lifestyle"

CAROL: Oh come on you're not some Stonewall hag from 1952
// Martin

MARTIN: I mean—my "plan" Carol I don't know—you tell
ME—what IS it? What the hell am I doing, I don't know

what to "plan" get a place in Chelsea and fuck people in it all day, is that a plan? //

CAROL: (It's more an itinerary but sure) //

MARTIN: Well I don't want to just fuck all right I want to fall in love. And I want reciprocal affection and I want to be *married*. And I know it means so *paltry* little to you, but it's what I *want*.

(Jerry starts to play his game boy at the table.)

CAROL: What you *want*? You *had* it.

JERRY: Gay people can fall in *love* // Martin

CAROL *(Grabs his game boy)*: (stop // that)

MARTIN: We can't get married—*not really*—because they— because *we're*—monsters evidently We need to be deprived of human connection—

CAROL: Well whining isn't going to help

MARTIN: I'm not WHINING if // anything I'm

CAROL: Maybe if you'd SHUT UP and take some ACTION for a change // you'd

MARTIN *(Deliberacy)*: But I've *taken*. *Action* Carol.

CAROL: What's that supposed to fucking mean.

MARTIN: You'll find out what it means.

(Jerry shifts uncomfortably. Smiles weakly—an attempt to leaven things, but is vanquished by all the bad vibes at the table. Carol casually takes a bite of food.)

CAROL *(Shifting tactics)*: So how long have you been harboring these feelings, have you always been gay?

MARTIN: I'm. I'm not sure.

CAROL: How could you not be sure?

MARTIN: It's a hard question.

CAROL: It isn't actually, when you fantasized about sex was it with a *penis* or a *vagina*?

MARTIN: Neither.

CAROL: Because you never had sexual *feelings*?

MARTIN: Everyone has // sexual feelings

CAROL: I'm just curious, when does it become a salient piece of information: "I'm gay."

JERRY: He was repressing // it

CAROL: I mean say in boarding school, when you two were in boarding school, you were post-pubescent then, so what were your fantasies?

MARTIN *(Flustered)*: I. I was busy—studying, I don't know.

CAROL: But what about when you weren't studying, like after gym class, in the showers, I've read stories.

MARTIN: I //

CAROL: Did you think of being penetrated? By a man?

(Pause.)

MARTIN *(Not looking at her)*: What if I did.

CAROL: Don't get angry // I'm just

MARTIN: Yeah so what. So men can be // penetrated

CAROL: I don't think it's a big *deal* I'm just asking: "*Have* you *ever* been *penetrated*? Do you ever think about that, being *penetrated*?" *(Beat, smiling nefariously)* This is like curling up with a good *book*!

[STOP]

MARTIN: And have you *noticed*, have you noticed how *gay* people, how we're not actually *real*?

CAROL: You didn't answer my // question

MARTIN: How we're like these *golems* these *monsters* //

CAROL: *Martin* //

JERRY: You're not GOLEMS // Martin

CAROL: YOU DIDN'T // ANSWER

MARTIN: How we're like these—*hairdressers* these people on sitcoms // it

JERRY: But that's //

MARTIN *(Spasm of real anger)*: I'm not your fucking hairdresser you know and it's like CUT YOUR OWN FUCKING HAIR.

(He slams down his fork.
Pause.)

JERRY: Now MARtin you're just, you're up*set.*

(Pause.)

MARTIN: But I'm not upset. I'm invigorated;
JERRY: Are you?
MARTIN: I'm elated. *(Pause)* Everything is just as it should be.
JERRY *(Drunk smile)*: Is it?

(Martin smiles warmly.)

MARTIN: "Hold up the glass" . . . right?

(Jerry smiles back reflexively. Then appears rather confused as he goes back to eating his stuffing.)

JERRY: The wha—?
MARTIN: The mirror. "Hold up the glass"?
CAROL: I'm still waiting for an answer to my *penetration* question but take your time. *(Beat)* Cute top by the way.

(Martin glowers at Carol. Jerry takes a big gulp of wine.)

JERRY *(Musingly, a non sequitur)*: "Love thy neighbor!"

(Carol gives him a dirty look.)

I'm just *musing* darling, jus' musing. Just . . . *cogitating* sweetheart. *(Playful revision)* EX-cogitating! *(Lifts a finger for emphasis)*

(Jerry eats. A short pause.)

CAROL: Actually it's "love thy neighbor as *thyself.*"
JERRY: Wha? Oh—well—that's a transLATION darling.

(She smiles diabolically.)

CAROL: But that's what it translates TO Jerry. That means you can *hate* your neighbor.
JERRY: Noooooo—
CAROL: YES you CAN that's what it en*dor*ses you can fucking *loathe* your neighbor as long as you hate your*self*! //
MARTIN: Actually in Christian theology it's "love your *enemy.*"
JERRY: That's true old man That's a good point—you *see* Carol Christ doesn't let you off so easy.
CAROL: *Where* does it say that.
JERRY *(Playful; wagging finger)*: Someone has been neglecting her scripture *darling.*

(Jerry rises from his seat.)

MARTIN: "And it was said, an eye for an eye and // a tooth for a tooth;"
CAROL: Where are you going Sit // down
MARTIN *(Impassioned swelling of feeling)*: "but I say unto // you:"
CAROL: Jerry //
MARTIN *(Pushes away from the table and stands)*: "resist *not* The Evildoers" //
CAROL *(To Martin)*: SHUT UP!

(Martin stands, a fervid prayer, a plea.)

MARTIN: "And it was // said thou shalt love thy neightbor"
CAROL *(To Jerry)*: Don't open that //

(Jerry produces a Bible.)

MARTIN: "and hate thine enemy! But I say unto you: *love* your enemies, *bless* them that // curse you,"

CAROL *(To Jerry)*: SIT down.

MARTIN: "do *good* to them that // *hate* you—"

JERRY: Don't be so *peremptory.*

CAROL: YOU OPEN THAT I'LL FUCKING SMACK YOU IN THE HEAD!

JERRY *(Opens the cover, smiling)*: Calm down darling—

(She smacks him. Hard. A beat.
Jerry turns the other cheek.
Carol sits.
Long pause.)

MARTIN *(Tiny smile)*: It works . . .

JERRY: What's that?

MARTIN: *Quarks.*

JERRY: What? Err—oh sure, yes—

CAROL: What the hell are *quarks?*

JERRY *(Innocently)*: They're little *particles* sweetheart.

CAROL: I KNOW WHAT THEY FUCKING ARE, I'M NOT—

[STOP]

(Frustrated, to Jerry) It's Thanks*giving*: I'm *preg*nant: we're having // a *ba*by

MARTIN: If you want to be authentic in your Thanksgiving: I mean what *is* Thanksgiving?

CAROL: GENOCIDE yeah I KNOW but I don't want to be *authentic* // Martin

MARTIN: But //

CAROL: I want to eat my Chambord cranberries and watch SPORTS!

[STOP]

MARTIN: You're so *American* //

CAROL: Yeah I AM "American"—and I *accept* it I *love* my country (and I know it's garbage but that doesn't stop // me from)

MARTIN: If you *really* embrace your country Carol you'd see that it has to break.

CAROL: "break."

MARTIN: Before it moves forward.

CAROL: Well that *won't* happen.

MARTIN: Really, it won't? Look at the Roman // Empire

CAROL *(Mimicking)*: ("the Roman Empire The Roman Em") —*have you ever read* GIBBON Martin? Do you know how LONG the Roman Empire in fact *lasted?*

MARTIN: Empires // fall

CAROL: It lasted for-fucking-EVER and they were HORRIBLY corrupt they had *slaves*, they—you know not everyone gets this swift comeuppance, that's storybook bullshit.

MARTIN: Should you be drinking //

CAROL: Rhetorical questions are accusations Martin // YES I

MARTIN: I //

CAROL: SHOULD BE DRINKING Have you ever been pregnant? how do you think women endure pregnancy, I feel like a marsupial, I hate my *pouch*, my hips are cracking open—

MARTIN: Do you *not* want to be pregnant?

JERRY: Carol //

CAROL: Where's my // pulpit!

JERRY: Carol the // baby

CAROL: OK: wait what's this:

(She starts reading from the Book of Revelation 9:2, a mock-sermon:)

AND HE OPENED THE BOTTOMLESS PIT; AND THERE AROSE A SMOKE OUT OF THE PIT, AS THE SMOKE OF A GREAT FURNACE: AND THE

SUN AND THE AIR WERE DARKENED BY—
REASON AND—BY THE—

(She stops abruptly—she falls against the table.)

JERRY: *Darling?*
CAROL: I don't feel right—

(Jerry runs to her; Martin is completely still.)

(Clutching her stomach) I don't FUCKING. FEEL
RIGHT—

(Snap blackout.)

3.

The following morning.
Martin and Jerry are both in their pajamas.
Breakfast.
Long silence.
Carol enters, fully dressed.

CAROL *(No affect)*: I'm going shopping.
JERRY: Darling . . . did you just . . . wake up or . . .
CAROL: I was doing the bills.
JERRY: Don't you think you should maybe . . . take it easy.
CAROL: I'm meeting Vera Wang at two, I'm doing that wed-
ding upstate.

(She gets her things together.)

MARTIN: How do you . . . feel?
CAROL *(Snaps)*: Maybe that's something you should ask *Judy.*

(Beat.)

JERRY *(Quietly, uncomfortably)*: Carol, Martin . . . was . . . just //
CAROL *(Glares at Martin, gelid)*: *When are you leaving.*

(Pause.)

MARTIN: I //
JERRY: He has nowhere to go Carol—he's //
CAROL *(Curt)*: OK *Jerry.*

(Resumes putting lipsticks and things into her bag.)

JERRY: What are you . . . going to—

(She exits, we hear the door slam. Jerry sits very still, dejected.
Silence.)

MARTIN: How is everything.
JERRY: What oh, delicious. Just delicious Martin thank you.

(Beat.)

I mean—I don't like poached eggs. But—
MARTIN: I thought—
JERRY: I really don't like anything. So—but I'll EAT anything, just put a plate in front of me: see? "mm, delicious!"
MARTIN: Would you rather have them scrambled, I could //
JERRY: No, no. it's just—I don't seem to like anything. I don't seem to have tastes.
(Short pause) Do you know: I keep a little notebook about the things I'm supposed to know, about Prokofiev, and what he did and William James and what he thought, but: I looked through my notebooks: I can't decipher *anything* I write. I mean I'm not kidding, it's like I've written everything in some kind of *cuneiform.*

(He laughs; then "bright":)

Gee, it's sort of interesting when you think about it old man: I mean you could draw out my complexity on a piece of *butcher* paper *(More frightening laughter)* with one of those those red—those *pen*cils, I mean //
MARTIN: It's sad to lose a baby.

(Jerry nods. Pause. Martin looks at him, deeply sympathetic.)

JERRY: Remember Roddy—he built that *bomb* in eleventh grade he was always reading that per*nic*ious literature?
MARTIN: What about him?
JERRY: Well now he builds bombs for a *living*, I ran into him //
MARTIN: Does he //
JERRY: Yes, that pig, he's in fucking MUNITIONS, the scum, and he makes an e*nor*mous amount of money, he works for the *gov*ernment. And I would have these conversations with him, late-night conversations—when he wasn't leafing through one of his pernicious little books which he nearly always was. And we would have these arguments about the nature of the "self." And Roddy of *course* didn't believe that people had selves, he didn't think there WAS a self! He accused me of being gram*mat*ical! And I would say, "Well Roddy, if there's no self who listens to the *Quadrophenia* album, day after day, tormenting us all with your fucking aha ha *Quadrophenia* album? who is this *person*, Roddy?"

(Pause.)

And now it's all these years later and I'm sure I have *no* . . . *idea* what I was talking about and I'm sure RODDY has the most fanTASTic little life making bombs and eating those fried things with powdered sugar with his little freckled twins off some coast of something or other, and I'm completely . . . lost. *(Beat; then sunny)* Well not *completely* lost ha ha, just, a bit uh, adrift, *(Manic convulsion)* JUST A LITTLE. *(Sober)* shall we say . . .

(Jerry covers his face. Pause.)

MARTIN *(Sadly, full of compassion)*: Jerry

(Martin goes to him, to console him. He wraps his arms around him. Jerry is very vulnerable. Jerry buries his face in Martin's shoulders. Martin is very moved. After a while, Martin lifts Jerry's head with his hands, he kisses the tears streaming from his eyes. Jerry lets him—it's the only love he's gotten in a very long time. Martin then kisses Jerry fully on the lips.
Jerry, disoriented, also a little disgusted, pulls away, uncomfortable—the trance is broken. This is too much.)

JERRY: No-no. *No* Martin.

MARTIN: OK.

JERRY *(Backing away)*: Unh-uh. *(Beat)* No.

MARTIN: OK I'm sorry.

JERRY *(Very VERY shaken)*: That's all right—th-that's— *(Contriving a smile)* perfectly all right Martin, it's—it's *natural.* I mean for *you.*

MARTIN: There's many different kinds of love. I'm. just learning.

JERRY: Yes.

(Pause.)

MARTIN: Or maybe there's *one* kind of love but in different pitches, different frequencies . . . You just have to know how to listen for it.

JERRY *(Very shaken, speaking quickly, anxious)*: Well it's *in*teresting, because—you know what li*bi*do is don't you

Martin well, *Freud*, you see, he had these *(Wiping tears, recovering)* these *int*eresting—ideas about libidinal *en*ergies—ca*thex*es he called them, I could—give you . . . literature if you . . .

(Silence.
As Jerry is speaking Martin grows more and more far-away, lost in contemplation.)

MARTIN: Do you know what the opposite of sin is? I thought it was virtue. But it's not virtue, do you know what it is? *(Jerry says nothing)* It's faith. *Faith. (Beat)* And you get it by having a principle. You don't have to feel anything. Real love has nothing to do with feelings. It's deeper than that. You don't even have to believe, you just have to perform a series of actions. "If you kneel down the faith will come." That's why I'm doing all this.
JERRY: Doing all what?

(Martin's face lights up; he looks at Jerry expectantly.)

MARTIN: Christian love . . . remember? *(Short pause)* Just now I was trying to help you by comforting you, but that's not help. That's just a band-aid. When you comfort someone, it's because deep down you feel there's no hope. That's how I used to feel . . . *(Moved)* But now I know there *is* hope. But I'm still—all this old fake *stuff*—I'm still try-ing to root it // out
JERRY: To *comfort* me is all right, Martin it's // just
MARTIN: No Jerry, pain is the best thing. *(Suddenly very focused, very intent)* You're at the portal and you're so scared but you have to enter into it. *(Beat)* If I were just an ordinary friend I don't know maybe I could leave it alone . . . But you're *everything* to me. *(Upset)* I won't let you die.
JERRY *(Perplexed; smiling)*: Die? I'm not dying.

(Martin looks at him with all the pathos and heartbreak one would feel toward a dying man oblivious to his own condition.)

MARTIN *(A wounded child)*: But . . . your soul is sick.
JERRY: My . . . *soul?*
MARTIN *(Quietly)*: I didn't know until I came here. But I know it now.
JERRY: My *soul* is . . . sick?

(Jerry laughs. The laughter builds. The more he laughs the more he wounds Martin, who looks on, helpless.)

MARTIN: Do you know I hated myself? That's why I chose my life. I chose a life I could hate so it could fit how I felt about myself. Is that what you're doing?

(Jerry's laughter dies down. The embers of a smile over the following:)

JERRY *(Lying)*: No.
MARTIN *(Rueful, deep sadness)*: Jerry;
  you haven't suffered enough
  or you wouldn't be lying to me now.
  (Very tender, sweetly:)
  I'm inside the molecules
  I can feel
  everything you feel,
  look at me:
  this is what you *look* like.

(Martin looks right at him. He weeps openly.)

JERRY *(Uncomfortable)*: Martin—please
  (Feeling increasingly bad for him) Martin . . .
  what are you . . . doing?

MARTIN: *Showing* you
  your *in*sides //
JERRY *(Uncomfortable)*: Well stop it
  (Stop; unexpected jolt of anger)
  STOP IT!
  (Then retracts; he goes to Martin)
  Martin *please* . . .
MARTIN *(Weeping)*: How do I stop? How?

(Jerry softens somewhat. He goes over to Martin, tentative, tousles his hair lightly. Martin lunges impulsively for Jerry, kissing him. Jerry pulls away. He wipes his mouth with the back of his hand.)

JERRY: Don't do that!
MARTIN: Why?
JERRY: Why, because it makes me fucking UNCOMFORT-ABLE buddy, *that's* why //
MARTIN: But isn't discomfort a good thing? without discomfort you couldn't grow or change, you can't be a whole PERSON //
JERRY: But uh, that's marvelous and everything like that but: I'm *married* you see I'm married to *Carol* //
MARTIN: Married?
JERRY: Yes // *married*:
MARTIN: You don't even know who Carol *is*. You have no cognizance // of
JERRY *(Unstable)*: Well, aha ha—OK but now—I mean I'm not GAY! I mean—orientation-wise, it's just, you know, it's not my THING. *(Pause; then quietly pleading)* We're FRIENDS that's important to me I *need* your friendship . . .

(Beat.)

MARTIN: I know . . .

JERRY: I lost a *baby*.
MARTIN *(Rueful)*: And it wasn't enough.

(Jerry looks at Martin, flummoxed and deeply hurt.)

JERRY: Don't do this; don't scare me like //
MARTIN *(Incipient violence)*: like what, am I a monster?
JERRY: I never said you // were
MARTIN: No—am I a predator? What am I? How can I make
myself *real* to you? What must I do? *What?*

(Jerry starts to exit, Martin pulls him back.)

JERRY: I'm //
MARTIN *(Raging, but profoundly helpless)*: Or—WHERE
ARE YOU GOING—or—NO maybe I'm something you
whipped out of the air Jerry like s-s-some pinwheel at a
carnival— Right?
JERRY: (no of course // not)
MARTIN: A MONSTER? a MONSTER Jerry Is that what you
want me to be?

*(He grabs Jerry violently and shoves his hand down
Jerry's pants. Jerry tries to push him off.)*

(Rabid) HERE! HERE!

*(Jerry finally pulls away from him. He's shivering, he's
out of breath. He tucks his shirt back in, not looking at
Martin.)*

JERRY *(Voice up a pitch)*: You have clearly ascertained // —er
MARTIN: I love you.
JERRY *(Trying to be "rational")*: —certain—feelings, feel-
ings for uh for *me* which I—

(*Martin pulls Jerry's face to his own and kisses him violently—Jerry not yielding as easily as he did in the previous attempt. There is something irreversible in this kiss, something ominous.*
Jerry finally gets away. He touches his mouth. There's a bit of blood.)

(*Betrayed*) You . . . hurt me . . .

(*A beat, then as the panic increases, the pace picks up breakneck speed, gets fast and out of control over the following:*)

MARTIN (*Innocent*): Did you want me to hurt you?
JERRY: You have to leave here.
MARTIN: Hurt me // back then
JERRY: I can't have this in // my house—not
MARTIN (*Quick*): You WANT pain you miss // the pain
JERRY: You have to leave // here Martin you
MARTIN: In your calves? you're *empty*
JERRY: have to go you // have to
MARTIN (*Childlike shame*): I'm *sorry*
JERRY (*Frightened; vehement*): GO! GO Martin LEAVE! YOU HAVE // TO
MARTIN (*Hysterical, a tantrum*): I'M SORRY Jerry I'M— (*Maniacally*) DON'T DO THIS TO ME (*Desperate retraction*) I'm sorry I'm sorry I'm sorry // I'm

(*Loud music cuts in as the style has tilted somewhat, gets manic, compressed. Over the following, Jerry holds his hands over his ears; squeezes his eyes shut. Martin touches him and Jerry jerks his body away, tramps to the opposite side of the room, turns to confront Martin—then squeezes his eyes shut. Martin lunges for him, desperate. Jerry jerks his body away, covers his ears, etc., etc.*)

JERRY: LEAVE YOU HAVE TO LEAVE HERE GET *OUT GET OUT GET* //

MARTIN: YOU'RE EMPTY Jerry I KNOW YOU! *I KNOW YOU!*

JERRY: *OUT* Martin GET *OUT GET OUT GET OUT GET* //

(They're both screaming at the top of their lungs, at top speed, overlapping one another, complete chaos. Lights cut off.)

4.

Sound cuts off. Lights up.
We are—for the first time in the play—in Jerry and Carol's bedroom.
An open suitcase on the bed, half packed.
Carol in front of the "mirror" (i.e., the fourth wall) wearing a fashionable—strikingly nontraditional wedding dress. She has a somber expression. The dress doesn't quite fit, but she looks beautiful in it. She contemplatively smoothes the silk over her stomach.
Jerry enters, puncturing this sort of trance she's in. He's carrying over the agitated, confused, frightened energy from the end of the last scene.

CAROL: You know actually there's a parity; we sort of look alike; she's a painter she went to—what's that school in Rhode Island.

(Jerry just looks at her.)

She's marrying another painter, they both have trust funds. *(Indicates the back of the dress)* See these? Chandelier pieces; Stella McCartney, they collect sweat. *(Pause)* I was just seeing what I looked like in— *(Pause)* Are you alright?

JERRY: Are you— //

CAROL: Excited for your trip, I'm packing your things
JERRY: Do you want to come with me.

(Beat.)

CAROL: To Geneva?
JERRY: Come with me.
CAROL: Don't be stupid I have work?

(Pause.)

JERRY: Martin's leaving.

(She turns to him.)

CAROL: How'd that happen.
JERRY: He . . . he wants to go.

(Beat.)

CAROL: I think it's a good thing.

*(She turns back, continues to adjust things.
Long pause.)*

JERRY: Please . . . uh p-please . . . need me.
CAROL: What.
JERRY: I'm not a threat to you. Am I. I'm nothing. Just—
CAROL: What are you talking about I know you're not a //
JERRY: I could never harm you . . .

(Beat.)

I'm nothing, I know I'm a complete nothing I know that
I'm just—baby a little baby I'm // a baby
CAROL: Stop this—why are you behaving this way?

JERRY: I just want a little pat on the head, a kiss on the cheek or something, I don't know.

CAROL: Can we talk about this later.

JERRY: I know it's . . . hard, but . . . if we //

CAROL: Don't be maudlin.

[STOP]

JERRY: Things fall apart // I mean

CAROL *(Playing with her earring in the mirror)*: That's a novel by Chinua Achebe //

JERRY: THAT'S NOT WHAT I'M TALKING ABOUT!

(Jerry has grabbed her arm, pulling it—it's a bit violent actually—away from her ear.
Carol looks at him. Seriously, quietly.)

CAROL *(Quiet but venomous)*: Don't ever touch me like that.

JERRY *(Penitent)*: You're my wife.

CAROL: I'm not you're wife you don't have a *wife*

(Beat.)

you have a well-stocked *liquor* cabinet. You have a *DVD* collection. You do not. Have. A wife.

JERRY: I'm right here.

(Pause.)

CAROL: There's a ghost in the room.

(Beat.)

JERRY: You think I'm a ghost?

(She looks through him. She returns to the mirror, contin-ues to put on her earring.)

(Despair) You think I'm a ghost? *(Beat; then rage)* HEY //

(He pulls her arm and swivels her toward him, violently.)

CAROL *(Breaking free of him)*: WHAT DID I JUST SAY!?

(Jerry is suddenly confused and frightened—by her as well as this odd passion consuming him.)

JERRY *(Somehow ashamed to say this)*: I . . . love you.
CAROL: Well . . . I love // y
JERRY *(Rage and pain mingled)*: But you're just speaking words. But I'm NOT. And I need. I need you to love me back I really. Need. That Carol—I really—I just—NOW.
CAROL: I don't
JERRY: NOW. NOW.

[STOP]

*(They eyeball each other for a moment—coiled tension. Jerry is breathing heavily. Music underscoring.
In a single gesture, looking right at her, he rips his shirt open. The buttons spill onto the floor. It is sexy and torrid and felt.
He approaches her. He grabs her face with his hands.
Just when we think he's going to kiss her he drops to his knees. In a single gesture, he grabs her waist with his hands, burying his head in her stomach, planting endless, hungry, penitent kisses. This is an act of grace. Carol is taken aback by this intimacy, and by Jerry's uncharacteristic ardor. She looks down at him; slowly, she lifts her hand to his hair.
The music bumps up.)*

5.

The following day. The Thernstroms' apartment.
Martin is moving out, he's getting together a last few things.
He's wearing pajamas. Carol is reading a magazine, sipping
coffee. She lights a cigarette. She's wearing the wedding dress
from the previous scene.

MARTIN: Where's Jerry?
CAROL: Do you have everything?
MARTIN: You look //
CAROL: It's for a client, Jerry's on his way to the airport //
MARTIN: He's //
CAROL: He has his conference.

(*Beat.*)

MARTIN (*Hurt*): Today?
CAROL: He was up packing early this morning, he said to tell
    you good-bye.

(*Beat.*)

MARTIN (*Distant*): Oh, that's right.
CAROL: Everyone's packing. Everyone's leaving, now I'm all
    by my lonesome. but that's all right. I have work //
MARTIN: Do you //
CAROL: a wedding in the country, a tall-grassed Valhalla,
    fresh-cut flowers. (*Beat*) and I have to catch up on read-
    ing and things. (*Pause*) Where are you going, do you
    have a place?
MARTIN: I'll stay at a hotel, I guess.
CAROL: Which.
MARTIN: I don't know, I'll look for something.
CAROL: You'll look for //
MARTIN: A hotel.

CAROL: Well I know a hotel, but didn't you make reservations?

MARTIN: I thought I'd just get in a cab and just eeny meeny // miney

CAROL: Do you want to call the Pierre?

MARTIN: The Pierre, no—I don't I don't think I could afford that.

CAROL: Well where are you going to stay? I really think you should call up and reserve first, the hotels will be all booked this // time of

MARTIN: I'll be fine.

(Pause.)

CAROL *(Reining in the impulse to control)*: Well you'll find something.

(Pause.
Martin returns to his last-minute packing.)

MARTIN: How do you feel?

(Carol looks at Martin.)

CAROL: Is there something in particular you'd *like* me to feel?

(Beat.)

MARTIN: Why do you say that.

CAROL: Because you keep asking me, "How do you feel?"

(Beat.)

MARTIN: I'm just concerned //

CAROL: Don't be; I'm perfect.

(Beat.)

MARTIN *(Sympathy)*: Well *(Beat)* It's sad to lose a baby.

CAROL: It wasn't a baby, it's not like—there wasn't anything, really, there wasn't anything to lose just a little glob the size of a nail clipping; it's like—blowing your nose or something—it's just //

MARTIN: But //

CAROL: Whoomp (and then a little blood but not much.)

(Beat.)

MARTIN *(Deep sadness)*: But . . . it could have been something.

CAROL: Yeah and a lot of things could have been a lot of things and they weren't.

(She lights a cigarette.)

You don't understand: I'm not sentimental. Sentimentality is noxious, do you understand that? It's a kind of poison.

(She drags on her virginia slim, eyeing his luggage.)

What is that, Pierre // Cardin.

MARTIN: I think:

CAROL: It's //

MARTIN *(Continuing, with some difficulty)*: I don't want to undermine what you're saying //

CAROL: Uh-huh //

MARTIN: because you're so smart about this kind of thing.

CAROL: "But"

MARTIN *(Gingerly)*: Don't you feel that perhaps you're not grieving because you haven't . . . *lost* anything.

CAROL: That's what I said.

(Beat.)

MARTIN *(Not cruel, honest)*: No, let me rephrase this: *(Beat)* You never *wanted* a baby . . . so if you lost a baby you never wanted in the first place, you wouldn't feel sad, you would feel: *relieved.*

CAROL: Why would I have a child I didn't want.

MARTIN: Why *would* you?

CAROL: Well I would answer you Martin but (a) you're being invasive and rude and (b) I did want the FUCKING baby so your question is *moot.*

(Beat.)

MARTIN: But you didn't.

CAROL: I did want the baby.

MARTIN: No.

CAROL: Uh—*yes*, actually, I *did.*

MARTIN: No . . .

CAROL *(Incredulous)*: Are you now *telling* me how I feel?

MARTIN: No. *You're* telling me how you feel. Only you're not *listening.*

[STOP]

CAROL: Don't be a blockhead //

MARTIN: I'm not a // *blockhead*

CAROL: Well you're being a bit of an idiot don't you think?

MARTIN: How did we get here.

CAROL: Where //

MARTIN: This—estranged—

CAROL: It's fine //

MARTIN: It isn't fine // something's

CAROL: Look:

MARTIN: come between us Carol and I // want to

CAROL: No something USED to be between us Martin *walls* I want them *back.*

(Pause.)

MARTIN *(Stung)*: That really hurts me.

CAROL: Well . . .

MARTIN: That's really hurtful, sometimes you. *(Beat)* Words can do violence OK? It's a kind of violence //

CAROL: Well what's a little violence between friends. *(Puffs on her cigarette glibly)* Right?

[STOP]

MARTIN: *You're so stuck //*

CAROL: I'm not // STUCK.

MARTIN: Circling in this terrible orbit //

CAROL: You're angry because we're kicking you out // alright, but don't

MARTIN: I'm not angry, no, just sad.

(Carol laughs.)

(Not angry) Is that funny?

CAROL: No—no—

MARTIN *(Musing)*: Maybe you never experience your own sadness, so you're uncomfortable with mine.

CAROL *(A little smug)*: Yes . . . that must be it, "Carol the un- feeling bitch."

MARTIN: You're // not

CAROL *(Barking)*: RIGHT?

MARTIN: unfeeling Carol, you feel everything; but your feel- ings appall you so—then you pretend they don't exist. You don't *listen.*

CAROL: I do listen.

(Carol grabs a glass of water and takes a sip.)

MARTIN: OK if you're listening what just happened.

CAROL: What?

MARTIN: WHAT DID YOU JUST *NOT* HEAR?

CAROL: Now you're just being crypto-annoying, I'll call the doorman // to take your

MARTIN: You don't *listen* //

CAROL: I still hear the crash of cymbals ringing in my head from the Berlioz concert two nights ago (I actually have a headache so) //

(She pops two advil.)

MARTIN: You did it again.

CAROL: What.

MARTIN: What just happened.

CAROL: I drank a glass of water. I drink glasses of water all the time.

MARTIN: What didn't you hear?

CAROL: I'm annoyed.

MARTIN: A certain clink of metal.

CAROL: What

MARTIN: Carol . . .

(Carol freezes for a moment. There's something ominous to it. She looks down at her hand. Lifts it to her face. No ring.)

CAROL: Where is it.

MARTIN: I'm trying to *help* you // OK?

CAROL: Where *is* it?

(Beat.)

MARTIN: I took it.

CAROL: Can I have my ring.

MARTIN *(Not punishing)*: I don't have it.

CAROL: Where is it.

MARTIN: I threw it in the East River.

[STOP]

(Carol laughs.
Martin laughs.)

[STOP]

CAROL: Martin, this is sincerely not funny, now come on, where's my ring.

MARTIN: I threw it away it was garbage by your own admission.

(Pause.
Martin nods, sadly, almost childlike in admission.)

[STOP]

CAROL: *YOU TOOK MY RING?*
MARTIN: Yes.
CAROL: With the garnets.
MARTIN: Look at your eyes.
CAROL: The invincible // band?
MARTIN: Your eyes are all red.

(Beat.)

CAROL *(Wounded)*: You're lying.
MARTIN: It was from love.
CAROL: Martin, *why* would you // do that
MARTIN: you said "it's too heavy"
    My hand, my heart, my life,
CAROL: I //
MARTIN: "I'm tired" //
CAROL *(Protesting)*: I'm NOT tired.
MARTIN *(Becoming very sad as he says it)*: "I'm . . . *sinking*"

CAROL (*Knowing he's right*): I'm . . . I'm not . . .
MARTIN: "free // me from the lie that is my life."

(*She massages the finger that held the ring, as if it were broken.*)

CAROL: I never . . . said that . . .
MARTIN (*Closes his eyes; an incantation*): Break Carol.

(*Beat.*)

CAROL: That's not going to happen.

(*She recovers control completely—or appears to.*)

MARTIN: It already did.

[STOP]

CAROL: We won't press charges or anything you'll // just leave
MARTIN: You just won't see it //
CAROL: And you'll never see us // again.
MARTIN: And until you do that, until you see it that's all you'll ever be //
CAROL: HEY.
THIS IS MY LIFE.

(*Beat.*)

MARTIN: It's not a life it's a shell.
CAROL (*Less sure*): And this is my // house
MARTIN: You're a shell, you said so yourself.
CAROL: I never said that.
MARTIN: You're *sinking*, that's what you // *said*
CAROL: You don't just cross the threshold Martin and walk into a person's home and say, "Fine, Carol's life, I'll WRECK it."

(She feels around her ring finger again, anxiously.)

MARTIN *(Sincerely hurt)*: Is that how you perceive it?

CAROL: HOW I // PERCEIVE IT?!

MARTIN: I can certainly // understand that point of view

CAROL: "HOW I"—THAT'S WHAT YOU'VE—just get out of my house, you know what //

MARTIN: And it's valid if you subscribe to a certain worldview (but my only // qualm—)

CAROL: What "worldview" SANITY it's not a fucking WORLD-VIEW it's the fucking SUBSTRATE of human exis-tence!!!! *(Icy; calm)* We won't press charges or anything. You'll just leave. Yes. You'll leave and we'll never see you again. *(Beat)* Do you understand? *(Beat; eyeballing him)* You will Never. See us. Again.

[STOP]

MARTIN: I //

CAROL: Leave, you're upsetting me.

[STOP]

MARTIN: Something's missing //

CAROL: Leave //

MARTIN: Carol: //

CAROL: I don't want to hear anymore //

MARTIN: But you do //

CAROL: LEAVE //

MARTIN: You want to hear all of it In the best smartest truest part of you you do want to hear it //

CAROL *(Fidgeting nervously)*: JUST GET OUT OF HERE!

[STOP]

"Jerry . . ."

MARTIN: He's not here.

(*Carol opens the front door of the apartment. She holds the door open for him.*)

[STOP]

Can I just //
CAROL: GO AWAY.
MARTIN: I just feel this is unfinished.

(*Beat.*)

Remember the apricots?
CAROL: What *apricots.*
MARTIN: The ones I gave you, well (*Beat*) I put something in them.

(*Pause.*)

CAROL: You what?

(*Silence.*)

MARTIN: I
Put something.
To
To cause you to . . .

(*Long pause.*)

(*Tenderly*) What's the saddest thing.

(*Carol begins to shake uncontrollably.*)

Is it losing something? Is that the saddest thing?
No.

(Beat.)

It's the loss of *loss*.
Right? It's
not knowing you've
lost anything
if you haven't experienced suffering you're *cursed*
do you see that?

(Beat.)

And I removed it
break.
It's OK, the curse is undone.

CAROL: You're crazy.

MARTIN: I'm // *not*

CAROL: You're crazy oh my god

MARTIN: Carol //

CAROL: *Don't say my name.*

MARTIN: I //

CAROL *(Weakly, desperate)*: "Jerry . . ."

MARTIN: Break, it's // OK

CAROL *(Sinks helplessly down to the sofa, she's not being rational)*:
"*Jerry . . . help me . . . Jerry . . .*"

MARTIN *(Tears; fervid)*: And that's what you were saying the
whole time: "help me" but no one heard your screams—
but *I* heard them; and I came to free you, to liberate
you from the *suffering* you didn't know was *yours*
(Beat) by . . . giving it *back* to you *(Beat)* Now it's yours
again.

*(For the first and only time in the play—possibly for the
first time in her adult life—Carol cries, and her crying
carries with it currents that eddy backward with the force
of her entire history.*

Martin, deeply moved, goes to her and hugs her lovingly and, oddly, protectively, as if he'd like to shield her from the pain that he's just inflicted on her.)

(Swelling with compassion) You think no one will ever know how terrified you are . . . But I DO KNOW.

CAROL *(Very tiny)*: You . . . *know?*

(Martin nods. She looks at him. As crazy as this is, something in him makes her believe that at that moment he's the only person to have ever seen her. The rage and exasperation are still there but slowly they are eclipsed by this absolutely bizarre tenderness—it's like a trance state. Martin holds her face with his hands. He kisses her on the lips and she lets him.
He kisses her again, this time it is more overtly sexual— it's not merely erotic; it is enormously complicated. Carol's pain is channeled into abandon as the kissing becomes increasingly heated, almost violent. Carol starts to scream. Martin gets more passionate, more violent.
He bites out her tongue.
Carol is screaming and thrashing—she backs away in shock. He realizes what he's done.
Horrified and confused—he spits her tongue out of his mouth in full view of the audience.
Carol stands there in shock—shaking uncontrollably, making inaudible little noises.
Martin's breathing gets heavier.)

MARTIN *(To himself)*: OK: what's my ethic?

(Pause.)

I'm in the m-m-molec . . .
(Weakly) I'm
I'm . . .

(He looks down at the extirpated tongue. A pause.
A horrified recognition; it has gone too far.
He starts to retch.)

Oh god.

(He covers his mouth.
Stops himself.
Slowly raises his gaze to meet Carol.)

No

(He can't look.)

No no no no no.

(He squeezes his eyes shut, shakes his head wildly, wishing
it away.)

HELP. HELP ME.

[STOP]

(Grasping at straws) No it can't be wrong—It's—

(He shuts his eyes, tries to concentrate.
Opens his eyes. Nods sadly, like a small boy.
He grabs a sharp knife from the kitchen.
He goes to the chopping block.
Carol sees him and starts screaming.
He cuts off his finger, weeping from pain. He holds up his
severed hand, the blood pulsing out. A nightmare.
A crack of thunder; the rain beats down.
Martin is still holding the knife.
Carol backs up, afraid for her life.
Carol runs to the door, runs out of the apartment.)

WAIT—

(Martin runs after her, leaving the door open.
Long silence.
Jerry enters with luggage. He's holding the mail in his
hand. He's sopping wet from the rain. He hangs up his coat
in the closet.)

JERRY *(Calls out)*: Darling, the new issue of *Harper's!*
Carol, the flight was canceled, the weather is . . .

(He mumbles the rest.
As he walks to the sofa, he slides on the waxed floors.)

(oh these damn . . .)
Carol??

(He sits on the sofa and opens the magazine.
He checks his watch. The storm outside is raging.)

Carol??

(He removes his jacket. Folds it neatly over the sofa. He sits
back comfortably on the sofa. He starts to put his feet up,
then just as they are about to land on the naked, sparkling
clean table he remembers *to take his shoes off, which he*
does, with élan—pleased that he remembered the house
rule. Puts them on the shoe rack. He goes to the bar and is
about to pour himself a drink. Just as he's about to pour—
he stops himself. He considers for a moment. He puts down
the liquor. He puts the glass back. He sighs. Moves back to
the sofa, sits. He put on his glasses and reads the cover of
the magazine.)

(Reading aloud) Salman Rushdie declares jihad on
HarperCollins . . .

(He's intrigued. He flips a page of the magazine gaily.)

(Sings, smiling as he reads:)

>You made me love you
>I didn't want to do it
>I di—

(A sharp crack of thunder cuts him off.
Blackout.)

Act Three

1.

[TITLE: "Breaking Up"]

A thunderclap—and the lights snap on. Judy and Jerry in Jerry's apartment.
A few hours after the end of Act Two. It's still raining.
Judy's hair—replete with the white shock from Act Two—is now a frizzed mess, echoing, but not too overtly, Elsa Lanchester in The Bride of Frankenstein. *She's wearing her best outfit— possibly a Chanel suit, but dusted with spots of ash and some burnt patches. She's clearly been in a fire. She's got a scrapbook with her. She seems—oddly—more lucid than we've ever seen her. Which is not to say she's entirely lucid—she's in the throes of deep inner conflict.*
Jerry looks as he did at the end of Act Two. He's got a bit of a stutter now. There's a box of empty liquor bottles by his side, and on the coffee table are a cheese board, a few used plates, some silverware, a box of marrons glacés.

The colors, clothing, etc., should be conspicuously muted here—no more bright colors, patterns. The pace is different here, too—it's more awkward, slower, more haphazard, more fraught. There's white noise in the silences, it's sort of viscid, thick.

JERRY: And you say you just *couldn't* find an electrician.

(Judy shrugs, gestures with her hands.)

(Doesn't know how to react—mainly to her hair) Judy
uh
uh—I mean—th-this is *terrible*; where are you going to
go?
JUDY: Well;
I mean—I came here.
JERRY: D-do you have any . . . money?
JUDY: I have a little in a bank account.
JERRY: Well—that's h-h-heartening.
JUDY: I have a trust fund. My mother controls it. *(Beat)*
I could stay with my mother. *(Beat)* Though to be hon-
est with you I hate my mother; she hates me too—we're
very . . . *symbiotic*—in our hate. *(Beat)* I'll probably have
a conversation with her about it at some point.
JERRY: That's—a shame.
JUDY: No, I've learned to embrace it.

*(Jerry nods encouragingly. Pause.
Judy leafs through her scrapbook.)*

JERRY: Well . . . you're—always welcome here you know.
JUDY: Am I?
JERRY: Of course darling, of *c-course* you are.

(Beat.)

JUDY: I have to say: I . . . *demured*—when I considered coming here Jerry. Because—isn't Martin staying here?

JERRY: M-m-n-
No—NO—no no—he h-h-h-

JUDY *(With purpose)*: Is he here? Because that would be awkward. Do you know he never insured the house? so now
I don't have a place to live. It's. *(Getting caught up in
the sadness. Beat)* But that's how women in third-world
countries live all the time;

JERRY: That's true Judy.

(Beat.)

JUDY: especially victims of genocide.

(Beat.)

JERRY: Well— // actually I think

JUDY: *Is* Martin here? It's alright, you can speak openly with
me, I'm a realist now.

JERRY: M-m-m- he's—uh—you know g-g-

JUDY *(Kind of annoyed)*: Jerry you're stuttering.

JERRY: N-n-not so mm-m-

JUDY: I can't understand you.

JERRY: Martin's g-g-g—he m-moved *out.*

JUDY: Why are you speaking this way?

JERRY: Oh. Well—I mean it could be—Judy I've quit drinking! I nearly forgot all about it. I spilled it all down the
drain—th-th-they say you experience withdrawal but
I'm—I-I-I'm I mean look at me—

(He holds out his hand, it's shaking wildly.)

(Surprised) Oh.

(He watches his hand shake. She does too.)

Well—it's not TOO bad is it?

(It shakes some more.)

JUDY: Jerry, may I be frank?

(Pause.)

Your—alcoholism has been an incredibly . . . destructive force; not only in my life, but in the lives of other people.

(He looks at her. She seems to be Judy, but is she?)

JERRY: Alcoholic? I—I wouldn't call myself that.

(Judy sighs.)

I—maybe drank a l-l-little bit more than I // should maybe

JUDY: NO you're actually an *alcoholic. Jerry.* And it's been taxing on *everyone. (Beat)* You always gave everything this sheen of fun? but there *wasn't* any fun. You demanded all the attention and then sucked the energy out of the room when you had it. it wasn't fun. You were incoherent—and I exerted a lot of effort in pretending to understand what you were saying—when you actually weren't making any sense! *That's not my fucking JOB Jerry!*

(Pause.)

I mean I. like you Jerry. I'm. Just trying to be clear about how your choices impact the lives of other people.

[STOP]

JERRY: I think this is—*tremendously*—exciting, Judy . . . *(She looks at him—surprised by his reaction)* you're exhibiting a—real—*intrapsychic*—*wellness* . . . it's really v-v-very heartening—truly.

(Pause.)

JUDY *(Now oddly fragile)*: Thanks for being so nice.

(Now that she's won she's plagued with guilt.)

Because it's
hard for me to articulate You know to
say what I
To say what . . .

(She tries to undo the crying but can't. Jerry pats her knee avuncularly, looks at her sweetly. He offers her a marron glacé—she doesn't notice. He eats it himself.)

Sometimes it comes out this way.
I'm actually very strong.

(Pause.)

I know how to fix it I think.
I'm much more lucid than I seem.

(Jerry nods, an analyst now. A contemplative pause.)

JERRY: Do you want to put on some m-*makeup*? Or.
JUDY: Because I thought about it and I realized, "Well Judy, at least you're not a *torture* victim, you're just divorced!" *(She laughs, a little too loud)* I'm in a good mood now, aren't you? I love the sound of the rain, I wish it would rain forever!

(Jerry smiles, a bit strained.)

JERRY: What's that book you're holding?
JUDY: A scrapbook!

JERRY: It's nice to k-k-keep scrapbooks Judy.

JUDY: It's been healing. Do you really see an intrapsychic wellness in me?

JERRY: You seem just m-marvelous Judy—you've really rebounded—do you want s-s-some lipstick or something Carol must have some // lying ar—

JUDY: No I don't like lipstick anymore. I don't see why women should have to disguise their faces for men. Men should be attracted to my face as it is. This is my face, and if men don't like it they can go *fucking rip out their eyeballs.*

(Jerry freezes, smiles a sickly smile.)

(Barely holding back tears) I'm sorry if I'm being inappropriate—but it's important to say what one feels. I think I'm becoming a whole person now.

JERRY: Well that's the important thing Judy, wholeness, I mean, it's just t-t-terribly important to be whole, and to find things that fulfill you at that deep errrrrrrr You know level. It's just m-m-marvelous.

(Long pause.)

JUDY: So are you excited Jerry?

(He smiles.)

JERRY: Ex*ci*ted?

(He looks at her.)

JUDY: About the *baby*!

[STOP]

(He freezes; the smile freezes, starts to crack.)

JERRY *(Not getting up)*: L-l-let me get you a drink // Judy.
JUDY: Oh, I'm not thirsty
JERRY: Are you s-s-sure?
JUDY: What's the matter? *(Pause)* Jerry?

(Jerry smiles, shrugs. An awkward moment. He starts to—nervously—pick out his eyebrow hairs.)

JERRY *(Seeing her face)*: What. Oh *these*: Oh HA HA: oh they just fall out! *Face* it Judy we're getting older: things fall out! A ha ha.

(He absentmindedly sprinkles the extirpated eyebrow hairs onto the floor, the sofa; then, instantly, realizes he's done this and—worried about the mess—tries to recover them.)

What about a snack—a little snack, perhaps a *marron glacé?*—You see Judy, they wrap them in these pretty gold papers I like that. (Don't you think that's *classy* Judy, *gold*—) Oh you have to try this . . . oh I think I'll have JUST one more, I don't— *(He stops. Looks over to her. A beat)* What's the matter, darling?

(He opens a marron glacé as he speaks—rather rapidly, lots of nervous energy.
Judy spots Carol's tongue lying fugitive on the floor. Judy moves closer, scrunching up her face, trying to make out what it is.)

What do you have there darling?

(Judy examines it a moment before responding.)

JUDY: Is . . . that a *tongue?*

JERRY *(Curious, furrowed brow)*: Tongue?

> *(Jerry picks up the tongue with a fork.*
> *Jerry puts on his glasses and examines it. He puts it on a*
> *plate and wiggles it around.*
> *He sniffs it.*
> *A beat.*
> *He turns to Judy.)*

Gosh. That's—kind of *weird.* Do you think it's a *human* tongue?

JUDY: What else could it be Jerry?

> *(They stare at it.)*

JERRY: It could be, well . . . who knows—a—*cat* tongue.

JUDY: Cat?

> *(Beat.)*

JERRY: Err *(Making it up as he goes)* cats always, well they— like to—c-c-c-creep around. Into. Those—pneumatic— *pipes* and things, right? maybe—uh. Who *knows* it . . . sort of creeped around uh into one of our pipes and— had an accident!

JUDY: Yeah I don't know.

JERRY: It's possible anything's POSSible—cats—*slink* around have you ever seen a cat—Judy—like this have you ever *(He does an imitation of a cat "slinking")* and then they sort of— *(More slinking)* they SLINK—they—I mean am I RIGHT?!—HAHAHA—they—th-th-th-th aha ha ha . . .

> *(Martin has entered the room—he is wearing nothing but*
> *his pajamas, now soaked. He's been standing there unseen,*
> *shell-shocked into silence, watching them.)*

Well anyway *(Excited)* HEY: are you hungry? because
we have some of this marvelous quince paste and some
of this really // just excellent Man*che*go artisanal—
JUDY: I'm really // not very
JERRY: from— *Oh* and we have these new knives we just
sharpened we have a nice runny *l'Edel de Cleron*! Oh and
the rind is *edible* too now how's //
MARTIN *(Blurt; a child)*: I hurt Carol.

(Jerry freezes.)

JERRY *(To Judy)*: What's that, dear?
JUDY: I didn't . . . say anything.

[STOP]

*(Jerry furrows his brow, considers. He shrugs and returns
to the cheese.)*

JERRY: You know Judy: *cheese* is the *corpse* of *milk*—did you
know that? there's—a Dutch biologist wrote a // whole
JUDY: I said I didn't want cheese.
JERRY: Well that's f-fine Judy, no one has to eat anything they
don't want to eat, that's a h-h-hallmark of civilized society.

(Beat.)

MARTIN: I—*hurt* Carol.

*(Jerry stops. He looks left, then right.
He turns, sees Martin. Stands.)*

JERRY: Uh.

*(Judy sees him now. Her posture changes, stiffens, her
comportment.
They look at each other.
Silence.)*

JUDY: Hello.

(Pause.)

JERRY: I—I—err. You haven't..*gone?* I . . . uh . . .

(Martin cannot make eye contact with him.)

MARTIN: She died.

(Pause.)

It was
like an orchid
The way her her
dress spread
In the river

(Pause.)

She just
kept . . . *sinking.*
I went in to get her but.

(Pause.)

I tried to . . .

(They look at him—utter stupefaction.)

[STOP]

(Jerry eats marrons glacés, and cheese, and anything he sees, and he smiles, and he nods approvingly. Martin just looks on at them. This goes on for a while.)

Carol // is

JERRY: Carol is d-dead Yes I heard. It's f-f-fine. It's perfectly *fine* Martin.

(Jerry eats, hums.)

(Mouthful of food) My god this Manchego is scrumptious—oh Judy you must try this it's so earthy! Just d-d-delicious!

(He stuffs his face. Smiles contentedly. Blocks it all out. He looks down at the tongue.
Beat.
Smile falls.
Beat.
Chewing stops.
Short pause.
Starts to retch—spits out the food on his plate.
Pause.
Looks around at them—smiles a strained smile.)

R-raw milk cheeses
a ha ha . . . You know h-how it

[STOP]

I must
clear off to bed: I'm
terribly
s-sleepy.

MARTIN: I learnt it wrong.

(Pause.)

(Can't look at him) I'm sorry.

JERRY: *Learn? "learn"?* I don't kn-kn-kn—

[STOP]

(As if this was a clever joke he didn't quite get) Ha ha ha ha—oh. *(He sighs)* You can make your b-b-bed Judy can't you the // sheets are in the

MARTIN: I couldn't . . . I—tried to //

JERRY *(Obscenely casual)*: Whatever you want to do is all right with me. *We do our best.*

JUDY: Jerry has promised me the sofa so I don't know if. It's *possible* but we would have to—forge—boundaries, certain— You really—should leave but the weather is so bad I don't—want you to catch cold. You look cold. You. *(She looks at him)* I don't want you to be . . . *sick*—I'll . . . change your pajamas.

JERRY: Good night.

(Jerry starts to exit for the bedroom.)

JUDY: Jerry he—he needs to—change into—

(Martin looks at her. Touches her face very sweetly, very sadly. She melts. She clasps his hand. He looks into her eyes very tenderly.
Silence.)

MARTIN: *We're dying.*

[STOP]

(Martin stands; looks down at the knife a few beats. Grabs the knife, cuts his own neck.
Lights shift. Time starts to warp, slow down.
A scream comes, faraway, hollow, distant. Jerry looks away. Martin holds his throat, drops the knife, collapses in slow motion.

Judy's face contorts into a frozen scream.
The sound of screaming enters her throat like a blast of
wind.
The world breaks open.)

2.

The scream gets louder, higher, reduplicates, multiple tracks,
pitches, timbres. A propulsive, savage machinery.
The sound gets louder and louder then abruptly cuts off.
After a few beats, we hear the droney sounds of a video game—
pong?
A few beats. Then the tiny glow from a game boy that Jerry's
playing.
A faint glow on Jerry. His denial has compounded. He's lost in
the game, giddy, quietly laughing to himself.
Judy enters with lit candles, places them throughout the room.
We see that Martin's body is sprawled on the sofa.
The rain and thunder are worse than ever—it's really coming
down.
Jerry's body is shaking somewhat from the DTs. His stutter is
worse.

JUDY: Where are they?

JERRY: (Oh I'll g-get you I'll—get you I'll—)

JUDY: Jerry stop playing that. *(Pause; she grabs it violently*
from him) STOP IT

JERRY: Oh—now you made me l-l-l-lose—you made me lose
the whole— *(Weird spin into violence)* GAME. GOD F-
FUCKING DAMNIT!

(Long pause.
Judy goes to Martin's corpse, feels his wrist—futilely—
for a pulse.)

JUDY: Where's the ambulance, it's been nearly an hour.

(Jerry looks over at her.)

The power's not //

[STOP]

I don't—*feel* right.

(Pause.
Judy looks around at the fractured landscape that was
once a living room. It's terrifying.)

Where . . . *are* we.

(Jerry is clearly panicking, but tries to hide it. He looks
around a bit.)

JERRY: Well—errr—we're in m-m-my h-house . . . this is
my—err—living room—th-th-there's just a bit of a
blackout—but—it'll all be . . . it'll b-b-be just—just—
j-j-just . . . er . . .

(As Jerry is speaking Judy has made her way to the win-
dow. Looks out. Freezes—it's ominous. Jerry sees her—
stops speaking. Everything goes silent except for the sound
of the rain.)

(Terrified) Judy?

(Silence.)

(Tears) It's . . . all . . . *flooded* //

(Jerry slowly, tentatively, makes his way to the widow. He
looks out.)

What are those . . . *floaty* things?

(Judy can't speak to respond. Jerry suddenly realizes they're bodies. Panic.)

Oh. oh—uh—

(He turns away.)

JUDY *(Terrified)*: Jerry—please—I don't know what to do, can you—help // me I
JERRY: OK OK—uh—let me th-*think*—
Judy
"I . . . *believe*."

(She stops. She remembers.
She turns, slowly, to him—
A tiny smile.)

JUDY: Tinkerbell?

(She looks at him.
She nods. She's a girl again, just for a flash.
She laughs—but too much . . . he laughs too without know-
ing why.
It stops.
A pause.
Back to the impossible reality.
She looks away for a moment.
She turns to Jerry. Something in her has died now.
She looks at him for a moment.
She kisses him on the forehead.
She crosses right in front of him, takes the knife off the
table. Looks at it.
A beat.)

JERRY *(Gingerly, frightened)*: Wh-wh-where are you going?

(Pause.)

JUDY *(Very sweetly)*: Play your game.
JERRY: B-b-b-
JUDY *(Sad for him)*: I'll be . . . right back.

(He looks to her, very afraid. He knows. She walks quietly in the bedroom—shuts the door behind her. He watches, helpless.)

[STOP]

(He retrieves his game. Tries to play. It's dead.)

JERRY: HEY—the battery w-w-w-
The—oh—FUCK
FUCK
FUCK.

(Pause.)

(A frightened whisper) Judy?

(He looks to the bedroom—he's thinking of going in but can't bring himself to see what's happened.)

Judy come quick.

(Pause.)

Carol . . . . are you in there?

(Fillip of panic.)

Judy stop tr-tr-tricking me it's not f-f-funny.

(He goes to Martin.)

This isn't funny old man now g-g-get up.
come on—let's get you a nice bath
Where's the gin.

(Silence.)

WHERE'S MY GIN.

(Pause.)

OK.
Oh.
Oh I see.

(Jerry laughs to himself, it's a bit nuts.
He plunks down next to Martin's corpse; turns to Martin.)

Well! *(He looks at him)* This is a ch-challenge.

(He laughs—but it's despairing. His body is shaking from
the DTs.)

[STOP]

(He sees a Bible.
Stops laughing.
Looks at Martin. Looks at Bible.
Gathers more energy around this.)

(To himself) you can undo it.

(He slowly picks up the Bible. Clasps it to him.)

Y-y you can—
YES YOU F-F-F-F-Fucking can.
You inflict the wound, you can't lance it *I* have to do that.

(Beat; increasingly fervid; he opens the Bible, eyes gleaming.)

I HAVE TO DO IT. I HAVE TO DO IT.

(He's shaking crazily, turning pages, frenetically, clumsily.
He looks at Martin. Stands. Puts on his glasses, hands
trembling.
Reads from Corinthians 15:52.
He starts slowly, tentatively.
It builds into evangelical zeal.)

> W-w-w-we shall not all s-sleep,
> but we shall all be ch-changed.
> In a moment . . .
> In the twinkling of an eye . . .
> at the l-last trump. for the tr-trumpet shall sound . . .
> and the dead . . .
> shall be r-r-r-aised
> inc-corruptible.
> and we shall be . . . ch-*changed.*

(He looks at Martin.
He waits.
He looks at Martin.
Nothing.
Nothing.
He looks away—starts to weep: he's totally lost now.
The lights change.
Suddenly—almost imperceptibly—a hand moves.
The hand lifts. We see it but Jerry does not.
Martin's eyes open.)

MARTIN: Jerry?

(Jerry opens his eyes.)

Hi . . .

(He slowly, cautiously turns to Martin.)

JERRY: M-m-m-m-
MARTIN *(Playfully)*: Hiiii Jerrry . . .

(Jerry covers his mouth with his hand and shakes; he's totally flustered, complete disbelief.)

JERRY: M-M-M-M-
MARTIN: It's *me.*
    Jerry it's me.

*(Martin sits upright—turns to Jerry.
He feels his face, chest: blood; laughs.)*

Oh; gee—I'm bleeding—don't worry I feel fine.
JERRY: M-m-m-m-m-m-m-
MARTIN: You're shaking.
JERRY: I I I I—
MARTIN: Scared?

(Jerry nods yes, like a child. He starts to weep—a deep release.)

Sshhhhh. it's OK, look, I'm here:

(Jerry nods no—he has a terribly worried expression—trauma.)

Don't be afraid: it *worked: look*—it all worked out, just as you said.

(Beat.)

You were *right* . . .
People *are* disconnected from their lives . . .

(Jerry looks at him.)

but You're a *whole person* now . . .
JERRY: I'm I'm—
MARTIN: The *fundaments* . . . right?

(Jerry looks at him—nods yes.)

JERRY: You're my f-friend . . .
MARTIN: *Right* Jerry?
JERRY: *Kn-know* each other
MARTIN: Want me to hold you?
JERRY: B-baby . . .

(Jerry—still tremoring wildly—nods yes frenetically.)

MARTIN: Yes, you're just a little baby aren't you?

*(Jerry laughs, he weeps in Martin's arms.
Judy enters wearing the wedding dress. Her hair is beautiful, the shock of white is gone. She is the Ideal Judy.
She sees Martin. Jerry looks up.)*

JUDY: Martin?

*(Martin looks at her, smiles. Jerry is panicked all over
again, turning to Judy, then back to Martin, again and
again, both frightened and amazed.)*

JERRY *(To Judy)*: Y-y-y-you— *(Looks to Martin, then back)*
He c-c-came back he c-c-c—
JUDY *(Incredulous)*: Martin?

(Judy smiles. She laughs joyfully. They all laugh.
This all has the tenor of a dream.
The wind gets louder outside. The storm gets more intense.
The walls start to shake.
Judy looks around—frightened.
The door to the apartment blows open.
Carol is standing at the threshold.
She stands there for a moment. Then enters—dripping
wet. She is something dredged up from Atlantis.
But something is different about her, aside from her
appearance, and slowly we realize what it is: she has devel-
oped the tragic, shattered nobility of someone who's been
stripped of all vestments of civilization.
Jerry is shaking with tears.)

JERRY: C-c-Carol . . . I was right—I was *right*: we fall and rise
and are *risen* l-l-like empires—Torn asunder, made one
f-flesh . . . b-broken, repaired. This is g-g-g-God's grace,
it is—I see it now.

(He shakes and tremors wildly.)

I I s-see it . . .

(Slowly, shakily, weakly and with some effort, Carol lifts
her left hand, her fingers slightly spread.)

CAROL: I'm Not Broken.

(On her finger is the ring Martin deposited in the East
River: miraculously retrieved.
The ring gleams.
As the lights begin to fade, Carol's patina of strength, as it
were, quickly starts to erode. Her lips quaver, the tears well
in her eyes. There's a deep, disconsolate sadness in her.

Jerry closes his eyes, smiling slightly, moving his lips; a garbled, fevered prayer.
Tableau.)

END

Elective Affinities

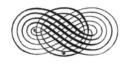

For Marian Seldes

Production History

Elective Affinities was commissioned by the Royal Court Theatre, and given a staged reading there in March 2002. The production was directed by Phyllis Nagy, with Jane Asher as Alice. It premiered at the Royal Shakespeare Company in October 2005, then transferred to the Soho Theatre in London the following April, in a production directed by Dominic Cooke, with Suzanne Burden as Alice.

Elective Affinities will receive its U.S. premiere in November 2011, at Soho Rep in New York City, in a co-production with Piece by Piece Productions and Rising Phoenix Rep. It will be directed by Sarah Benson, with Zoe Caldwell as Alice. The design team will include: Louisa Thompson, set; Susan Hilferty, costumes; Mark Barton, lighting; Matt Tierney, sound; Tom Taylor, production stage manager.

Alice stands alone, addressing the audience. A chair, a tea service, a plate of expensive chocolates. She's very wealthy, dressed opulently—she's of the Brooke Astor, Gloria Vanderbilt ilk—almost of another era. She's very charming.

ALICE *(Chatty, very conversational)*: And so he asked us, "Are you going with something big or something small?" And John said well maybe small is best, because then it won't take up much space. And I said, no it's got to be *big*, because the *world* is big, and I want to see that bigness in the confines of this *one* room in this *one* house; I want it confined to *one room* the vastness of all the world, every latitude and longitude imaginable, I want it squeezed into *one* shape, and I want to look at it whenever I *want*. And John was just *galled*—and he stormed out of the room with his briefcase. And the artist, he sort of gulped, he was a little daunted I could tell, but I think it turned out all right. I mean, we're pleased with it. I mean, it's this very big, black, hulking . . . *mass*. It's a little terrifying. We're sort of . . . afraid. Of it. And John is very cross with me.

(She regards the sculpture.)

It seems sort of African to me. Or *Iberian*, maybe. I've never actually been to Africa. Or Iberia for that matter.

(Beat.)

To tell you the truth, I've never been anywhere, not outside my own country. But I've been to *museums*, I've been to *lots* of museums. I like museums better than I like art! I think they're very civilized. I've never been to Africa, but I've been to the Guggenheim. People say to me but you seem well traveled and I say, I *seem* it, but I'm *not*. I read books and I watch movies. But I don't like airplanes. I prefer to stay where I am and have the world come to me. It's very arrogant I know; I'm *terrible*.

(Beat; then excitedly:)

Oh, and I watch the *nature* channel—have you ever watched that? You can see animals eat each other *alive*! *(She laughs maniacally)* Can you *believe* it, they actually show this—I mean, it's almost *pornographic*! And, it's not just insects or grasshoppers, but big bloody animals, with tendons coming apart, and blood and gore, my *god*.

(Pours tea into a cup.)

My husband, John, he travels a lot. He's in Japan right now doing business. He's very cross with me, as I said— he doesn't like that thing—that's what he calls it "that thing." Or sometimes "das ding"—he's German so sometimes he says it in German—and that's how it is in German, "Das ding."

He's afraid of it, John is. A few nights ago he said to me, "Alice, it's growing, I think it's growing." I told him he was being silly. He said, "Either *it's* growing, or I'm *shrinking*." You know, Germans are such fraidy cats, they really are. The Germans themselves have a word for this.

(Beat.)

I don't know what it *is*, but I'm sure there is one.

(Adds sugar and milk to tea.)

Maybe they don't have a word for it—I don't know anything anymore. So John is cross with me, everyone is so cross around me, but people are just peevish these days. I mean, don't you find that? That people are so peevish? For example my girlfriend Deirdre—I mean I love her and we've known each other for ages—but she just got *very* recriminatory with me at a dinner party. She said— and she tends to get very annoying when she drinks, I mean she can really get on your nerves—she said, "But Alice: how can you justify what you said last week at the benefit about the *tor*turing of political *pri*soners. I mean can you really justify the use of *torture* on political *prisoners?*" And I said, "I *wasn't* justifying it." And she said, "Well, *Alice*, I'm not sure I understood your position. I mean, maybe I misunderstood your position, but from what I gathered you seemed to be really excited about the tor- turing of political prisoners, and what's *that* about?" I said to her, "Look Deirdre: who wants to use torture? *No one*, that's who. *Nobody* does, it's *unpleasant*. I was merely stating *fact*. I was merely stating that torture *would* be used. That the FBI could, should and *would* use it and that they *will* use *torture*. That's just how it is. And that *any* democracy in a ticking bomb situation would do that, that's just how it is."

She said, "A ticking bomb situation—what's *that*?" I said, "You know, like in those films, those horrible action films, when someone plants a bomb on a bus and you have a limited amount of time to defuse the thing but don't know where it is, and you've captured the bomber, and he won't tell you. What are you going to do then?

"I'll tell you what you're going to do: you're going to *torture* that man! *Anyone* would—to find out how to *defuse* it? *Anyone* would do that."

"But I could *never* torture *anybody*."

"Not even if your husband's *life* was at stake?"

"No."

"Or your daughter or your grandchild, not even then?"

"No," said Deirdre. "I could never. Torture. *Anyone*."

(She takes a short pause, then rolls her eyes. Takes a sip of tea.)

Ezra Pound, you know, that *poet*? He called the space between the two wars "a parenthesis of peace." Isn't that quaint sounding, "A *parenthesis* of *peace*." I love that. Where are we now, do you think? Mid-sentence?—or no, mid-paragraph, mid-*volume*?

I don't know where we are.

My mother used to read his cantos to me before bed. You know, those *cantos*? I didn't know what anything meant, but I *loved* it. My mother was a very great woman. I know everyone says that about their mothers, but in her case it was true. I had a very happy childhood. I remember during World War Two I asked my mother, "Why are we at war?" She said it was simply because men liked war, that they liked it better than any other subject—they liked wars, violence and sports.

I don't have any children myself . . . I wanted to—and we tried for a while—we did *try*. And then after a while we stopped trying—or *I* stopped trying. John kept trying, he was testing his, oh, mascu*lin*ity or something. But I surrendered. I accepted my fate. You know, like one of those gazelles, in the jungle, or the woods, or wherever the hell gazelles live. But it's incredible, really, when they're captured by some predator . . . they just sort of tilt their heads back . . . like this:

(She slowly tilts her head back and a little to the side.)

And this look of peace comes over them, in their eyes, this very . . . peaceful look . . . they're saying *yes*, I accept my fate—*yes*, I'm resigned to the fact that I'm going to die . . . and I accept that.

(She's gotten a bit dreamy and faraway, maybe even a bit sad, but snaps out of it.)

That was me! I was like one of those gazelles. I accepted my fate and—well that's a very dramatic analogy—I actually have a very nice life. I mean, *I* think it's a nice life.

(Beat; she pops a chocolate in her mouth.)

Or maybe it's horrible. Maybe it's a *horrible* life and I just don't see how horrible it is. But—I mean I *feel* happy. I've always considered myself a happy person. I've always *been* happy, I've always loved life. People say to me, "But you're so rich, you must be spiritually empty." And I say, "But I've managed to find spiritual fulfillment in material *things*." For example this tea—now I know this is going to sound dumb, but I just love tea, I love *this* tea—and when I drink it, I feel edified *spiritually*. I really do.

(Takes another sip.)

It's from Japan, this brand of tea. John brought it home for me—and it's just unbelievably good; and the flavors, they have names like "good times" and "swing time" and—ha ha—"time of your life" or, or "happy *ride*"— something like that I don't know . . . They don't correspond to any flavors in life, like peach or lemon. It's called "tonal systems." Isn't that a funny name?

(Takes another sip.)

OH—do you know that *ride*, that *teacup* ride? In *Disney World?* Have you ever been there? We went last year, and—say what you will about Disney, and *Lion King*— "hakuna makata" and all that but—really it was so much *fun*. We just *loved* it, una*bash*edly, we were like two pimply kids. And the teacups are—and I don't know if you've ever seen them—they're just so whimsical. They're *huge*ly oversized and you sit inside them and spin around. I love just spinning and spinning. And the children are like little cubes of sugar being stirred around and around . . .

(Beat.)

But I'm getting off track now—what was I . . . oh *yes*, the ticking *bombs*—that's right. Now Deirdre, you must understand, she's a very well-meaning person, she's well intentioned, so you can't hate her when she gets really stupid on you. And we're having this incredibly circular argument—"Don't you think it's sort of *bad* to torture people?" "But Deirdre Darling I'm not advocating torture." "But Alice Darling it sounds like you are, and we live in a democracy and don't you think we need to protect our democratic *ideals*?"—and as she was saying this they were playing a nocturne of Chopin's, whom I

(A nocturne plays softly.)

love to pieces, so I half listened to her and half to the Chopin.

(As Deirdre:)

"And is it really all right to violate certain ideals with the intention of upholding those ideals, I mean do you really think that's *OK*?" And I said, "*Well* Deirdre, if you *want* to live in a civilized society, then I guess it *has* to be OK, doesn't it." And she turned this sort of ugly pink color. And she said, "But that's not civilized *behavior*."

(Beat.)

And I said, "Well, I think *I'm* civilized. I mean I *try* to be nice . . . and funny, and smart—I mean, I'm a nice person, don't you think so Deirdre? Don't you think *I'm* nice? Don't you like *me*?"
And she sort of tilted her neck back, and she said of *course* she liked me and not to be ridiculous. And I said, "Because *I've* always liked *you*. Because we're *friends*. And you would never torture *me* and I would never torture *you*. Because we're *friends*. And she said, well that's true. And I said, "I would never harm you, Deirdre, or anything you loved. Because we're friends and we love each other. And love is preferential. I *prefer* you to other people." I said, "I'm with you right now because I'm rejecting billions and *billions* of other people. I'm rejecting them so I can make space for *you*. And our friendship is meaningful precisely because I reject all these other people. You can't love everyone—except in a general way, and love is too important to be generalized."

(Music fades.)

I thought I expostulated quite well.

(Beat.)

I mean *I* thought so.

(Picks up her teacup and sips.)

But I mean this whole discourse on human rights—the whole thing is sort of a joke, isn't it? I mean what sort of conversation *is* this? "But we have our *rights!*" As if *all* human beings have some innate value. As if we're these precious jewels, or individualized snowflakes or something idiotic like that.
I mean does anyone actually *believe* this to be true? or do we just *pretend* to believe it? and if we all are pretending to believe it—*why* are we *doing* it? I mean "I'm a horrible person" yes I *know* that but I'm *sorry*. I mean the gall, to assume that just because we're *human* we have these *rights*. Yes, it's nice to be *nice* to people, yes, absolutely; it's nice to treat people well, I'm not saying people should be mean to other people. But my god, the laziness, to just *assume* we *all* have some innate value . . . that this is just some *given*.
I mean, look: if someone flies in an airplane—is it their *right* not to crash? Do people ever say, "Oh, their rights were violated, their *human rights*, because they *crashed*." No, they don't say it because when you're up in the sky— flying around like that—you're defying *nature*.
And nature is very cruel.
Nature confers no *rights*.

(Beat.)

I mean, the *hubris*!

(Short pause; she crosses her legs—they are nice legs—she may be showing off a bit. Smoothes her stockings.)

I like hosiery a lot. If I had my druthers I'd buy a box of pantyhose every week.

(Beat.)

I don't really know what druthers are, do you? Anyway, I doubt I have mine.
HA HA HA HA.

(Sips tea; then overly casual:)

So!
That's my situation in a nutshell. Deirdre is cross with me, and John is cross with me too. Oh, John is *furious* with me. He thinks I've become "monstrous"— did I mention that? Well he does, that's what he told me. "Alice," he said, "you are becoming a monster. "Oh am I, John, that's so very interesting," I told him, "as if your forefathers weren't gassing Jews by the millions in the death camps."

(She laughs wildly at this. Then a short pause.)

Maybe that was monstrous of me, to say that to him.
It was, wasn't it.
It was very mean.
But maybe that's what you need to be when you're pro-tecting the thing you love. I love my husband, I love my friends. Other people, I'm indifferent to them.

(Beat.)

Until they harm me. Until they harm someone I love, or threaten to. Then I'm not indifferent. Then you bracket your normal way of living. Then it's war. You can permit horrible things, torture, murder, genocide and that sort of thing.

(Beat.)

And everyone is so cross with me, but that's what I think. They say, "We don't know what to say, we're grief stricken over what's happened, we're stricken with grief, we don't have the language"

(Then angry:)

But I *do* have the language and I am *pithy* and *precise*: Eliminate them! Take up the cudgels, and don't cry, and don't hang your head.

(Soft, trancelike, almost evangelical:)

Kill them, kill every last one. Kill every living thing, so nothing remains, *nothing*, nothing, kill *every*thing, kill *everyone*, then sow the earth with *salt*—sow it up like they did with Carthage—so nothing grows there ever *ever* again.

(After a short pause; smiles brightly.)

My mother used to say that to me. About relationships— we were talking about marriage I think. And she said that even the most intimate relationships, no matter what—your husband, your children—that these were all triangles. That there's no such thing as a couple, that there's always a third person. There's always someone who's *necessary* to the relationship but also *excluded* from it. Love, she taught me, is double sided. So to speak. So I suppose I do care about foreigners, political prison-

ers, murderers, terrorists—I believe they have value—
not innate value, but the value I assign them. Inasmuch
as they are the other side of my relationship with the
people I love.

I'm indifferent to *those* people and that indifference is
what makes it possible for me to be partial to other people. I think that's what love is.

(She glances over at the sculpture.)

"Das ding."

The Germans have all these words for things that in
America we don't have.

(Beat—then to us:)

I mean it is sort of horrifying.

(Pause.)

But I do think it's a work of art.

END

David's plays have been produced or developed at the Sundance Institute Theatre Program, the Public Theater, Lincoln Center Theater, the Royal Court Theatre, the Royal Shakespeare Company, Yale Repertory Theatre and the Woolly Mammoth Theatre Company. His play *Marie Antoinette* will receive a world premiere in a co-production by Yale Rep and A.R.T./Harvard in 2012. Other upcoming premieres in 2011–2012 include *3C* (Rattlestick Playwrights Theater) and *Elective Affinities* (Soho Rep). David is currently under commission by Lincoln Center, Berkeley Repertory Theatre and the Royal Court. He was awarded a 2011 Guggenheim Fellowship, the Whiting Writers' Award, the Kesselring Fellowship, a Steinberg Playwright Award (the "Mimi") and the Bush Artist Fellowship, among other awards. His as-yet-untitled memoir is forthcoming from HarperCollins. David is a member of New Dramatists, MCC Playwrights Coalition and Rising Phoenix Rep. He is a graduate of Sarah Lawrence College, the Iowa Playwrights Workshop and the Juilliard School.